What Poets Used to Know

Poetics • *Mythopoesis* • *Metaphysics*

What Poets Used to Know

Poetics • Mythopoesis • Metaphysics

Charles Upton

ANGELICO PRESS
SOPHIA PERENNIS

First published in the USA
by Angelico Press / Sophia Perennis
© Charles Upton 2016

Series editor: James R. Wetmore

For information, address:
Angelico Press
4709 Briar Knoll Dr.
Kettering, OH 45429
angelicopress.com

ISBN 978-1-59731-171-7 paperback
ISBN 978-1-59731-172-4 cloth
ISBN 978-1-59731-173-1 ebook

Four Anglo-Saxon riddles
Translated by Michael Alexander,
Reprinted by permission of Penguin Books, Ltd.

The poetry of Lew Welch
Reprinted by permission of City Lights Books

Cover Design: Michael Schrauzer

For Lewis Barrett Welch (1926–1971)

CONTENTS

Preface

POETRY, in our time, is not only a misunderstood art, but one that has been subject to a systematic program of denaturing and falsification, at the hands of those Andrew Harvey has characterized as "official tastemakers who have outlawed the sublime, and . . . a contemporary poetry world addicted to cheap irony, unearned despair, bizarre pastiche, narcissistic confessionalism, and blindingly boring baroque word games" [from Harvey's introduction to *Diamond Cutters: Contemporary Visionary Poets in America, Britain and Oceania*, Tayen Lane, 2016].

Poetry, as defined in this volume, is not entertainment. It is not self-expression. It is not propaganda. It is not a way for any particular group to define its identity or push its agenda. It is not an exploration of the colors and textures and odors of language in and of itself, apart from questions of meaning. It is not a celebration of terror and trivia in roughly equal amounts. It is not a costume. It is not a role. It is not a juggling act. It is not the triumph of verbal nihilism, nor a magician's technique for the misdirection of attention, nor any other form of assault upon—or betrayal of—human, natural or spiritual truth.

Poetry is a way of knowing based on the cultivation of *symbolic* or *anagogic* consciousness, expressed through the medium of human language. The games it plays are not sporting events but serious hunting expeditions carried out in the face of collective hunger and impending mass starvation. As such, it is a key to the vast treasure-house of lore and knowledge amassed by the human race over many millennia, a knowledge that remains locked in the vaults of verbal and mythopoetic symbolism. It is also one of the royal keys to the language of dreams, which make up perhaps a full third of human life. Without the ability to form and read symbols, to which the art of poetry provides access, it is virtually impossible to grasp the workings of one's own mind, and thus to come to any sort of realistic or practical understanding of *what a human being is*. And in view of the fact that we actually are human beings, what more disastrous form of ignorance can possibly be imagined? This is why poets have traditionally been the mystagogues, the psychopomps, the keepers of the Lore Hoard, the "unacknowledged legislators of the human race."

On the other hand, words are weak; someone who goes to meet a situation requiring any degree of subtlety or courage armed only with words is courting serious defeat. Why? Because it is possible to divorce words from *truth* on the one hand and from *action* on the other, and because all the Principalities and Powers of the Darkness of This World are dedicated to suggesting and enforcing this double divorce. Words can only overcome the ever-present danger of fatal weakness when three different criteria are met:

(1) When they are backed up by the full weight of meaning, by which I mean objective truth;

(2) When this truth has been paid for in full, thereby giving the speaker the authority and the right to speak it, seeing that it is impossible to be as good as your word if your word is better than you are;

(3) When the words are spoken in an intrinsically appropriate context, one in which their meaning and authority are not squandered on relatively worthless goods, or simply thrown away, but rather used to purchase something of real value: the full attention of the interested listener to something actually worth listening to. Such contexts are hard to come by these days; it is the rare poetry reading that can provide the same contextual integrity that the rituals of poetic theurgy and courtly praise of the heroes did in former ages. In our time, the true occasion for the poem will often appear at unexpected moments, and sometimes must be caught on the fly.

In this book I do my best to open the vaults of anagogic knowledge, lay out the laws of mythopoetic symbolism proper to the art of poetry, and point the reader toward the sources of traditional content proper to these intrinsically human ways of knowing—a truly vast territory—as well as defining the skills and techniques that poets have employed throughout the centuries to hunt and catch this knowledge and drive it deep into the human soul, on several levels simultaneously, thereby allowing us to know certain things *in essence*, as if by taste, before we even know that we know them. The truths we learn by the anagogic method are not mere aesthetic or psychological window-dressing; they are essential to the integrity of human life on earth.

Language is the central function of the human being; its anagogic role is to lead our consciousness beyond the limits of the sense-world by the process of *naming*. To witness the objects of both the world and the psyche in terms not of the generic categories they occupy but of their intrinsic identities is to transfigure them. It is to view them in the mirror of what the Buddhists call *shunyata* or "voidness"—that which reveals their transcendence of literal definitions—and of *tathata* or "suchness"—that which unveils their uniqueness and incomparability. The language of animals is utilitarian rather than symbolic; it has to do with whether or not a given object is physically present, and if so how it might be avoided or exploited; it deals in signs relating to what is going on now in the immediate environment rather than symbols of the Always So. But human language is fully symbolic, and consequently possesses the power to invoke the essential qualities of things, whether or not they are present in space and time, or can be used to satisfy immediate or future needs, or are designed to occupy physical space at all. But insofar as symbols fulfill this anagogic function, they become signs again, though in a different sense: instead of indicating what is present in the physical world, they *make* present, to human consciousness, realities of the spiritual world.

Every *truth* is both a recognition and an act; consequently there is no truth without a seer-and-speaker—a principle that applies even to the Creator of the universe. A book also has one or more seeing speakers behind it, and thus represents a record of human perception confirmed and established by acts of human conception. But once machines are given power over language—once words begin to appear that are spoken by no-one, not even in the silence of the human mind—then language inverts. It becomes not an outward sign of an inward meaning—in other words, a *sacrament*—but rather a draft levied *against* meaning, a phenomenon of debt rather than value, a raid on the treasury of human thought. For us to turn our language over to "artificial intelligence" programs, allowing it to be manipulated by algorithms rather than invoked by human acts of perception and conception, and fully paid for by the sacrifice that each such act requires, is therefore an unmitigated disaster; it represents nothing less than the betrayal of the human form. This is why it is of vital importance for us to regain at least some idea of what poets used to know, and thereby understand the sacred trust laid upon us by the power of human speech. The following essays are part of my contribution to this effort.

Introduction

THIS BOOK contains virtually everything I've written on poetics and poetic tradition that is not to be found in *Shadow of the Rose, Hammering Hot Iron, Folk Metaphysics,* and *Day and Night on the Sufi Path* (though some excerpts from the first book are included), as well as several pieces of "literary criticism". This criticism takes three forms: the analysis of the function of image, music and meaning in various poems; the indication of more or less explicit metaphysical doctrines that can be found in the works of certain poets; and the metaphysical hermeneutic of *mythopoesis*—the practice of "making *myths*"—which I like to define as "stories that are always true." I also have some things to say about the fundamental elements of the craft of poetry and their use in several poetic traditions. About 30% of this book is excerpted (and revised) from other books of mine; 70% is entirely new.

Mythopoesis—whether in speech, image, choreography, or the language of gesture known in Sanskrit as *mudra*—is essentially a dramatization of metaphysics; likewise metaphysics may sometimes appear as an exegesis of mythopoesis. Metaphysical truth can be spoken, painted, sculpted, danced or sung; the combination of these modes comprises, in the profane dimension, theatre, and in the sacred one, ritual and liturgy. The primary vehicle for metaphysical truth is the *symbol*, which is a higher order of reality, a higher order of *synthetic particularity* and *concreteness*, than a given discursive metaphysical proposition or discourse—which, vis-à-vis the symbol, will always be relatively abstract. For this reason, one concrete symbol can give rise to many possible abstract exegeses, just as it can sum up the entire spectrum of meanings contained by these exegeses in a single form. As for poetry, it is the most compact and self-radiant vehicle in the realm of language for the rendering of symbol: a synthesis of density and light.

Those capable of crafting poetry and being moved and informed by it ("informed" in the sense of "formed within") tend to have a more-or-less specialized configuration of soul, though not a particularly rare one. The Hindu Vedanta analyzes the human form in terms of the five *koshas*, the "sheaths" of the *Atman* or Absolute Indwelling Witness: the physical sheath or *annamaya-kosha*, the energy-sheath or *pranamaya-kosha*, the mental sheath or *manamaya-kosha*, the wisdom-sheath or *vijñanamaya-kosha*, and the bliss-sheath or *anandamaya-kosha*. Emotions are generated through the interaction between the mental sheath and the energy sheath, whereas the power of metaphysical expression, including metaphysical poetry, arises from the interaction between the wisdom-sheath and the mental sheath; language fulfills its highest function—the enunciation of *certainty*—when the mental sheath acts under the direct influence of the wisdom-sheath. In the psycho-spiritual and psycho-physical makeup of poets, the border between the energy-sheath and the mental sheath, and/or that between the wisdom-sheath and the mental sheath, tends to be relatively thin and permeable. These two permeabilities have both positive and negative effects. The mutual interaction between the energy-sheath and the mental sheath produces poets like John Keats, who are adept at expressing the feeling-tones generated by thought, as well as in understanding the conceptual implications of feelings: "Truth is beauty, beauty truth." On the negative side, this two-way open door results in the tendency of feelings to obscure thought, and of thoughts to generate impulsive emotional reactions. As for the higher permeability, that between the wisdom sheath (the Platonic *Nous*, the Scholastic *Intellectus*) and the mental sheath (the Platonic *dianoia*, the Scholastic *ratio*), this interaction, since it allows for the articulate expression of eternal metaphysical principles on the plane of language, produces meta-physicians and theologians, as well as metaphysical poets like John Donne: "Death, thou shalt die!" In negative terms, an excessive permeability between the wisdom-sheath and the mental sheath creates a condition where language acts as a barrier to the realization of Wisdom in the very act of expressing it—a barrier represented in the *Odyssey* of Homer, strangely enough, by the figure of the cyclops Polyphemos (see "Homer, Poet of *Maya*", below). Words swarm around Wisdom like moths around a candle and interrupt its light.

Introduction

This book is designed as a synthesis of poetics, literary criticism and metaphysics; when it succeeds most completely these three will be indistinguishable. It is also threaded through with poetry—not only verse itself, or accounts of various traditions where poetry and spirituality intermingle, but also with poetic textures, rhythms and inner correspondences—with an immanent energy that is always pressing the discourse to *be what it says* and *become what it knows*. Through this we can see that poetry, at its best, is a standing, walking and breathing challenge to the speaker to be as good as his word, to the listener to become as sharp as her ear—which is why, if we fail at these tasks, we will fall into *the world of words*, the hell of unreality. In the words of W. B. Yeats, "In dreams begin responsibilities."

A Course in Mythopoesis

What Poets Used to Know makes up one-seventh of a *mabinogion*, a Welsh word denoting a mythopoetic training-manual for aspiring poets. The other six-sevenths are:

(1) *Hammering Hot Iron: A Spiritual Critique of Bly's* Iron John, by Charles Upton (Quest Books, 1993; Sophia Perennis, 2005)—on poetry, mythopoesis, Jungian psychology and the warrior tradition.

(2) *Who Is the Earth? How to See God in the Natural World*, by Charles Upton (Sophia Perennis, 2008)—the roots of pastoral poetry.

(3) *Shadow of the Rose: The Esoterism of the Romantic Tradition*, by Charles Upton and Jennifer Doane Upton (Sophia Perennis, 2008) —the metaphysical roots of traditional romantic poetry and the medieval romances.

(4) *Folk Metaphysics: Mystical Meanings in Traditional Folk Songs and Spirituals*, by Charles Upton (Sophia Perennis, 2008)—the perennial metaphysical and mythopoetic tradition, from the folk through the literati to the sages.

(5) *The Wars of Love and Other Poems*, by Charles Upton (Sophia Perennis, 2011)—the beast itself.

(6) *The Ordeal of Mercy: Dante's* Purgatorio *in Light of the Spiritual Path*, by Jennifer Doane Upton, ed. by Charles Upton (Angelico/

Sophia Perennis, 2015)—a metaphysical, mythopoetic and psycho-logical exegesis of the middle section of the greatest poem of the western world.

In earlier ages, among many peoples, poets were the repositories of the total knowledge of their nation or tribe. The poet was the priest/shaman who acted as *pontifex* ("bridge-builder") between the divine and human worlds. Orpheus, for example, the primordial poet of the Greeks, had the function of mediating between the celestial gods of the Apollonian order and the cththonic deities of the Dionysian one; in this he resembled Hermes, the god of language, the premier psychopomp. For poets to claim such a role in our own times, however, is problematical—and the fact is that such claims are most often made by poets who have failed in their art. Not only has the outlook of the human collective become secular to the point where such pretensions are considered implausible (if not evidence of mental illness); even in the sacred dimension the function of the poet has long been superseded by that of the prophet, the priest and the mystic. God may still inspire poets, but He no longer chooses to employ them as the central interpreters of His Will among men. Nevertheless, no-one who lacks an understanding of what poetic knowledge is, how it functioned in former times, and what it can teach us today about the nature of human consciousness and our place in the cosmic order, can be considered fully informed as to the Way Things Are. Therefore I offer this book, along with its six companions, as an attempt to throw some needed light on this extensive dark spot in contemporary human knowledge. If the sleep of reason begets monsters, the sleep of symbolic consciousness begets super-monsters, like the "shadow-walkers" Grendel and his Mother in the Old English epic *Beowulf*—the dark beasts of false psychology, false philosophy and false religion: but wherever true knowledge is cultivated, such darkness cannot enter. In specifically poetic terms, these ogres may be taken to represent the dangerous chaos of the poet's own unformed material, bristling and seething with potential deception as well as hidden truth. These are the adversaries he or she must pacify, by the power of the poetic craft and the grace of God. May this book strengthen all true poets in that work.

⁓ 1 ⁓

Poetry, the Siege Perilous

This essay is adapted from the Introduction to *The Wars of Love and Other Poems*, Sophia Perennis, 2011

ONCE upon a time, poetry was a sacred art. It was immensely more "liturgical" than we can easily imagine nowadays, and dedicated to a double purpose: Memory and Theurgy. As Memory (the Muses being "the daughters of Memory") it carried not only the chronicles and legends of the great deeds of the kings and heroes of former ages, but also the history of the creation of the universe, its unfolding from the Night of the Unseen—its history, and therefore its structure, since the "history" of universal manifestation is that of a descent along the Great Chain of Being, the story of the "motion" from Eternity to Time—just as the *apocatastasis*, the restoration of all things in God, is the story of the re-ascent of that same Chain. (This is why, for example, we call our ancestors "Grandfather, Great-Grandfather" etc.: in traditional cultures, earlier times were considered to reside on an ontologically higher plane than later ones; whatever *preceded* us in time was seen as having *precedence* over us in being.) Any competent poet would carry with him a vast body of lore, representing the whole spiritual inheritance and much of the technical inheritance of his entire culture, stored in his naked memory.

As Theurgy, poetry called upon the Powers resident on the Great Chain of Being, in the name of the High God Himself, both to accomplish the will of the Deity and to fulfill the needs of human life, in terms of mating, food-getting, war, healing, and *knowing*. Theurgy combined in one skill what later became split into the two poles of *magic* and *prayer*. (This theurgic quality is still clearly discernible, for example, in the prayers of St. Patrick.) It was prayer in the sense that it called upon God, to praise Him, contemplate Him, and pray Him to fulfill legitimate human petitions; it was magic in that it called up the deepest psycho-physical Powers of the Human Form, as well as those Powers residing in the surrounding world considered as the *Shakti* of that Form (or in Blake's terminology his Emanation), in order to shape and release those petitions, often at great psychic and physical risk to the poet himself. According to Sir Thomas Malory, there was one seat at Arthur's round table—empty at the beginning, but destined in the end for Galahad—called the Siege Perilous, the "perilous seat"; no-one who was not absolutely pure of heart could sit upon it without injury or death. This legend led me at one point to define poetry itself as the Siege Perilous, and to characterize it further, paraphrasing William James, as "the moral equivalent of human sacrifice." The literary conceit of the Siege Perilous may in fact be derived from the Welsh legend of the stone seat on the mountain Cader Idris where a person, if he were foolhardy enough to sit in that chair over-night, would stand up the next morning either dead, mad, or a poet. But nowadays we have magic without piety, and (all too often) prayer without power. When poetic Theurgy broke down, the magical aspect became Promethean, if not Satanic, while the prayerful aspect moved in the direction of ineffectual sentimentality. And somewhere between these extremes fell the art of poetry, which—though it sometimes pretends to magic and is often infected with sentimentality—seems no longer to possess the virtues of either prayer *or* magic; it has become purely "recreational".

So poetry used to be a sacred art; but when a sacred art degenerates, it begets monsters. That's why it is probably safer to practice the art of poetry without any spiritual pretensions. But I did not avail myself of that precaution; consequently I was forced to process the toxic psychic residues of forms of the Sacred based on archaic revelations whose informing spiritual essences had long since departed from this earth. René Guénon, in *The Reign of Quantity and the Signs of the Times*, wrote that "persistent psychic influences, when deprived of the 'spirit' which formerly directed them, are reduced to a sort of 'larval' state, and can easily by themselves react to a particular provocation, however involuntary it may be . . . the influences in question can be quite pernicious enough, even when they are simply left to themselves." Seeking lyric inspiration through psychic explorations of the "collective unconscious" is just such a provocation; I can attest to the truth of this from my own experience.

Central to the traditional practice of poetry in the west is the concept of the poet's "muse." This presupposes a male poet who draws his inspiration from a subtle feminine presence, somewhat on the order of a Tibetan yogi's *dakini*; some of the troubadours, for example—like Dante—composed their songs and poems in honor of the Virgin Mary—at least after the Albigensian Crusade "re-Catholicized" Southern France. As is well known, the Greeks had nine muses, of which three—Calliope (epic poetry), Erato (love poetry) and Euterpe (music and lyric poetry)—relate to the art of poetry as we understand it. And given that the archaic Great Goddess overshadowed the entire Celtic world, it is clear that the Bards composed and sang by Her power and for Her ears before all others (a theme echoed in the traditional Scottish ballad "Thomas Rymer")—perhaps in Her aspect as Brigit, Goddess of Eloquence, Mother of the High God Ogma Sun-face—Brigit being analogous to the Hindu Sarasvati, patroness of knowledge, culture and the arts, *Shakti* to Brahma the Creator: the Goddess of *Creativity*. For the lyric poet, the arrival of the Muse or Goddess produces a peculiar psychophysical reaction, a spontaneous and uncontrollable hyperventilation designed to raise his subtle nervous system to the vibrational pitch where the words of his Muse may be heard and understood—*inspiration* precisely: the poet's Muse *breathes his poem into him*.

In the context of a living religion that allows for poetic inspiration and understands it, the poet's relation to his Muse is a conscious craft, hedged about with many traditional safeguards. In our time, however, the realm of poetic inspiration has fallen into the underworld of the "collective unconscious" where those safeguards are no longer available; consequently Brigit or Sarasvati has been transformed into Kali. In other words, to the degree that clear spiritual knowledge, emanating from the pneumatic plane, has become delusive spiritual glamour, residing on the psychic plane, the poet's

11

Muse must increasingly appear in the guise of the Goddess of Death. The poet susceptible to infernal glamours is under the power of illusion—the central core of that illusion being his own poetic ego—and the function of the Goddess Kali is precisely to destroy illusion; this is why so many poets, who have been left with nothing to worship in modern secular society but their own egos, are led to self-destruction: alcoholism, drug-addiction, suicide.

Originally poetry was both an art and a craft, two words that were once nearly synonymous. When the meanings of these words diverged, however, *craft* carried most of the original burden, denoting the acquisition and practice of a technical skill which, if a sufficiently high degree of proficiency were attained, might flower into true inspiration, after the technical aspect of the craft had become "second nature". (Any true musician will understand what I mean, most likely because poetry in its original practice was inseparable from music, just as both poetry and music were closely related to dance—as, for example, with the tribal Africans or Native Americans. The prosodic unit of a poetic line is still called a "foot", recalling the time when poems were danced as well as sung.) But when poetry began to be considered more an art than a craft, the word *art* degenerated until it came to denote a work produced primarily through inspiration rather than craft competence, an inspiration that the poet could only hope would somehow bring its own crafted verse forms with it, directly out of his or her sensitive poetic soul, through which the "cultural collective unconscious" might, on rare occasions, find a way to speak. (How like the Protestant Reformation is this passage from poetry as a craft to poetry as an "art", a change that's strictly analogous to the breakdown of the sacramental order—a true spiritual craft tradition—and its replacement with charismatic preaching—an entirely hit-or-miss proposition.)

Poetry was taught as a true craft in the Bardic Academies of Celtic Europe. While the apprentice poet was learning *prosody*, the science of poetic forms, he was at the same time stocking his capacious, pre-literate memory with *lore*—myths, legends, histories, technical knowledge of many different crafts (astronomy, meteorology, medicine, herb lore, gem lore, divination etc., and at least the symbolic aspects of metallurgy, agriculture, hunting, fishing, navigation, pottery-making, carpentry, masonry . . . poetry is built on metaphor, and every craft has a metaphorical dimension), as well as an encyclopedic knowledge of traditional symbols expressed, mythopoetically, in terms of images. He might also, in shamanic mode, become master of the subtle technical craft that would allow him to attain various states of ecstasy or "altered states of consciousness." Other cultures, of course, had analogous institutions. Persian poetry, for example—like that of Jalaluddin Rumi—also possessed many bardic elements in that it relied upon a vast stock of known and memorized traditional symbols, as well as drawing part of its inspiration, at least in Islamic times, from the ecstatogenic techniques of the Sufis. (For insight into the bardic aspect of Persian poetry, see the 15-volume encyclopedia *Sufi Symbolism* by Javad Nurbakhsh, particularly volumes One and Four, dealing respectively with the symbolism of wine and of the parts of the Beloved's body, and with that of the natural world.)

Strangely enough, if any group in contemporary North America still practices what might be legitimately called a "bardic" craft, it is the Old Regular Baptists. Since they have the whole Bible nearly memorized, they possess a large stock of traditional symbols ready-to-hand (or tongue). Couple that with the ecstatogenic technique of hyperventilation-while-preaching, and a deep and pious faith in the inspirational and wisdom-giving power of the Holy Spirit, and you have, in the form of a traditional *ex tempore* sermon given by the hardshell Baptist preacher, or other preachers of similar denominations, many of the elements of the traditional practice of bardic poetry. (Allen Ginsberg claimed to have developed the idea of the "breath unit" as his version of the poetic line, a line whose length is determined by the poet's lung-capacity, like the musical line of a jazz trumpeter or saxophone-player—but without a doubt the Baptists got there first. And those Black jazz musicians probably got it from their Black Baptist preachers in the first place.)

Under the bardic system, every poet was both the member of a school and the inheritor, practitioner and transmitter of a body of traditional knowledge—or rather traditional *wisdom*, a word that denotes theoretical knowledge become practical, information transformed into skill. But when the bardic academies of northern and western Europe fell apart, or were shut down, poetry was forced, by passive cultural decay and/or active persecution, to become an individual art. The broken academies released waves of wandering, out-of-work poets—jugglers, mountebanks and *jongleurs*—*proto-bohemians* precisely, who carried with them (like the Gypsies?) all the marks of a disinherited priesthood. (Who was Allen Ginsberg, after all, but a fallen rabbi, an unemployed prophet? And who is Jack Hirschman, past poet laureate of San Francisco, but a freelance Hasidic kabbalist turned poet, because he could find no place in his formerly-Jewish tradition to be anything else? The Hebrew prophets themselves were often the products of prophetic "schools", like the one on Mount Carmel—but as Simon and Garfunkel sang, back in the 1960's, in these days "the words of the prophets are written on the subway walls.")

So now we poets are forced to be individual artists with no stable patronage, freelancers who must hope somehow to access an inspiration that we have no formal method of relating to, and can't even really define. And whatever our poorly-conceived "inspiration" or shapeless "craftiness" happen to turn up we must immediately pimp out to a public that increasingly doesn't care, or (in the United States) to the National Endowment for the Arts and other funding sources, who will pay a tiny pittance to a miniscule percentage of us to act the role of poets in their nearly-meaningless pageant of "national high culture".

San Francisco poet Jack Spicer once said, "I write for the dead"—they being his only stable and reliable audience. As for myself, I apparently write for an invisible "tribe" who has never assembled; or for the dead, the ancestors—though it was never my intent to beguile them with my own uncertain talent, but rather give them a living voice—and, finally, for God alone, remembering Jack Kerouac's exquisitely pungent line: "God is the only critic who cares little for style."

Ever since the French Symbolists, if not before—ever since poets began to turn to the lurid underworld of the "unconscious" as the source of their inspiration, as well as to the vision of the natural world as seen from the standpoint of that unconscious, sometimes via drug-use—poetry in Western Europe and America has increasingly become a vector for a kind of infernal glamour (Poe; Baudelaire; Rimbaud; Lautreamont; Georg Trakl; the stories/prose poems of Dylan Thomas; Galway Kinnell's *Book of Nightmares*, etc., etc.)—a late modern phenomenon that is now in the process of being replaced by the infernal *glamourlessness* of post-modernism. In terms of Dante's *Inferno*, our culture has sunk below the sodden or fiery upper circles of Hell, and come to rest in its frozen depths. And on its way—on the road from infernal glamour, which is actually a kind of inverted Beauty, to post-modern deadness—it embraced at one point the deliberate pursuit of the ugly, as has been practiced by so many poets since the 1970s. And although this tendency is certainly still with us, it has begun to give away to a kind of post-modern, sub-factual nihilism, a barrenness of severed details unrelated to any deeper meaning whatsoever, whether archetypal, psychological, social, or natural. The "positive" quest for ugliness has turned into a totally negative *flight from meaning*, based on the very real fear that ugliness (since it is inseparable from Beauty, being Beauty's corruption) might actually *mean* something from time to time.

Nonetheless, in its original theurgic-mnemonic function and stature, poetry can be numbered among the final reverberations within the soul of God's creative act. The poetic art extends the Divine creativity far and wide within the human psyche, both individual and collective; it carries that Truth out of which, according to the Noble Qur'an, all things are made, to its ultimate psychic limits—in other words, as far as the threshold of unreality, evil, and non-existence. This is the great danger of poetry, to both the poet and the society around him, and the reason why the practice of it, outside of a traditional liturgical context, carries inevitable spiritual perils—as witness the alcoholism, drug addiction and suicide of so many poets in modern times. Poetry is the language of the gods. The poet, however, is not a god but a man—a man who has, as it were, stolen the Divine fire, the ability to create *icons*, living images of truth. If his skill is great enough, these icons will inevitably command belief—not in the form of assent to clear and true doctrine, but in terms of the kind of emotional and intuitive allegiance that only clear and true doctrine deserves. Consequently, if the iconic forms wrought by a poet are not objectively true as well as subjectively convincing, he has arrogated to himself the godlike power to *determine what is true by saying it*, and perverted that power. Only God can legitimately say what is to be true; if a poet attempts to do so outside of His inspiration and permission, he has become what Plato, in the *Republic*, calls a "liar." And this is a form of demonic invocation. In the words of the Qur'an, from the *surah* "The Poets":

> *Shall I inform you upon whom the devils descend? They descend on every sinful, false one. They listen eagerly, but most of them are liars. As for the poets, the erring follow them. Hast thou not seen how they stray in every valley, and how they say that which they do not? Save those who believe and do good works, and remember Allah much, and vindicate themselves after they have been wronged?*

To *say* something but not *do* it is to extend the name and image of Reality into imaginative forms that one has neither the power, the integrity, nor the *right* to realize. It is to create phantasms, to go into debt to Reality Itself, and thereby to wrong oneself, sometimes mortally. Poetry is boast, only action is proof; the poet who vindicates himself after having wronged himself is the one who has paid, with spiritual warfare and suffering, the debt he incurred when he arrogated to himself the Divine power of creative speech—and has thereby become an honest man: a man *as good as his word*.

～2～

Image, Music, and Meaning

EZRA POUND, in *The ABC of Reading*, defines the three integral dimensions of poetry as *phanopoeia*, *melopoeia* and *logopoeia*. Phanopoeia is the power of poetry to make us see images with our mind's eye. Melopoeia is the music of poetry, its volume, pitch, pace, texture and rhythm. And logopoeia is poetic statement, what the poem declares to be true, either universally, personally, anecdotally or imaginatively: X is always true; X is the way I say I am, or she is, or it is, either right now or at all times; X is a specific, reportable event that happened to me, or she, or it, one that took place yesterday, or is happening presently, or will occur tomorrow, or happened once in a vision or a dream—all these are examples of logopoeia.

When it comes to phanopoeia, the real master may well be the Japanese haiku-poet, Bashō; here are three famous poems by him:

> An old pond—
> Then a frog jumps in,
> Kerplop!

> The sea darkens—
> A wild duck's call
> Faintly white

> A wild sea—
> In the distance
> Over Sado,
> The Milky Way

In these poems the melopoeia is overwhelmed by the phanopoeia; all is sacrificed to the Image, which imprints itself on our minds with a force both subtle and somehow shocking. As for the statement-level, the logopoeia—"I hear a frog; I hear a duck; I see the stars"—it is completely subsumed into the Image. We do not hear a man describing his experience; we see only the experience itself, as if there were no experiencer at all, or as if we were the actual experiencer, able to look through someone else's eyes, just as we can see through our own. Here we encounter the Buddhist doctrine of *anatta*, "no self", expressed in terms of the *shunyata* (voidless) and the *tathata* (suchness) of phenomena. Things possess "suchness", are precisely as they are, because they cannot be fully rendered in terms other than themselves; and because there is no real essence "inside" them and apart from their appearance, they are void of self-nature. When the seer realizes *anatta*, the things he sees becomes void. The practice in this sort of phanopoetic writing is to clear the poem of "I saw the beautiful sunset and this is what I felt about it", so that only "sunset" remains—either that or the poet's feelings have to become so objectified that (so to speak) they become part of the sunset itself, not part of the poet sitting there having feelings about it. Who wants to plow through somebody else's personal history—or one's own, for that matter—to get to the Thing Itself?

Japanese art, including haiku, is traditionally used to render four different qualities or "ontological moods":

(1) *Sabi*—"It is what it is"—*suchness*.

(2) *Wabi*—"Down-to-earthness"—the "uncarved block" of the Taoists.

(3) *Awarë*—"The long good-bye"—poignancy, nostalgia, the primal human reaction to the Buddhist *anicca*, the doctrine and fact of impermanence.

(4) *Yügen*—"Shock of cosmic Mystery"—*satori*—the sudden Awakening to the truth of things.

In the frog haiku, *sabi* and *wabi* predominate; in the duck and the Milky Way haikus, *yügen*. Note also the *synesthesia* that turns the quacking of ducks into a visual image with a particular color; the phanopoeia of this haiku is so powerful that it transforms even a sound into an image. Synesthesia is actually quite common in human perception; if we don't recall experiencing it, that's probably because we were never taught to look for it. Imagine the sound of a celeste; who would ever think of a sound like that as a being a deep red color? The music of the celeste is white, yellowish-white, bluish-white, but certainly not red. Likewise nobody would think of the sound of a tuba as being white; it is gray, brown, reddish-brown, bronze, but never white.

As for melopoeia, which includes meter, rhyme, assonance, alliteration, and many subtler effects (such internal rhyme and half-rhyme), the poets known for mastery of this aspect of the art include Gerard Manly Hopkins, Algernon Charles Swinburne, Dante Gabriel Rosetti, and Dylan Thomas, among many others. (I hesitate to include Rosetti and Swinburne, however, since they—especially the latter—are sometimes suspected of being all music and no substance.) Keats and many others are masters of melopoeia, as indeed any competent poet must be, otherwise why is he or she writing in verse instead of prose? And Lew Welch worked hard to make us hear the music, or the interesting texture, of common American speech, as in his test-line "duffer coat equivalent to parka." If you can hear the music in that line, feel the "chewiness" of it, then you've got an ear for American speech and can learn to appreciate all sorts of melopoeia that are not "musical" in the sense that (for example) Italian is often said to be. American poetry, as opposed to English verse, is sometimes called "percussive"—and drums and cymbals are certainly musical instruments, every bit as much as the piano or the violin.

In the poetry of Dylan Thomas, his astounding melopoeia often eats up all the phanopoeia and logopoeia that try to compete with it, disgorging them only later after it has long finished incanting and we begin to come back to our senses, or to our other senses. One of the best examples of the dominance of melopoeia in Thomas, or in English verse as a whole, is his poem *Altar-wise by Owl-Light*; here is his first stanza:

> Altarwise by owl-light in the half-way house
> The gentleman lay graveward with his furies;
> Abaddon in the hangnail cracked from Adam,
> And, from his fork, a dog among the fairies,
> The atlas-eater with a jaw for news,
> Bit out the mandrake with tomorrow's scream.

19

> Then, penny-eyed, that gentlemen of wounds,
> Old cock from nowheres and the heaven's egg,
> With bones unbuttoned to the half-way winds,
> Hatched from the windy salvage on one leg,
> Scraped at my cradle in a walking word
> That night of time under the Christward shelter:
> I am the long world's gentleman, he said,
> And share my bed with Capricorn and Cancer.

Images are certainly here, many of them, but they are tossed together and apart like the wreckage of a three-master broken by the storm, then cast up on the beach of our attention in a pile of flotsam made of oak and cork and hemp and brass fixtures and human limbs. That's the phanopoeia. And as for the logopoeia, is there any of it there somewhere under that gleaming pile of rubbish? What in hell does the poem *mean*? It appears to be as non-representational in terms of words as an expressionist canvass is in terms of stroke and color.

This poem is not just an animal howl, however, or the sound of an air-hammer or the crashing of the sea; its images, half-images, doubled and tripled images are not merely there for the sound of them; they are there for the *logopoeia*. In other words, we will never grasp the purpose or the *excuse* for them until we understand their symbolism:

Altar-wise: in a sacred manner, though with a contrary wisdom
(*altar* and *alter*)
By owl-light: by the inner light, through the dark night
In the half-way house: in this world between birth and death
The gentleman lay graveward: the gentleman slept the sleep that
leads to death
With his furies: accompanied by his nightmares.
Abaddon in the hangnail cracked from Adam: the Devil was cloned
from a fragment of Man—
And, from his fork: and from his crotch, his fuck
A dog among the fairies: sprang the hell-hound/ prowling the wood
of the faggots, the wood of the harmadryads;
The altas-eater with a jaw for news: the geopolitical predator,
devouring history's nightmares

Bit out the mandrake with tomorrow's scream: tore up Man like a
  root from the earth / and unveiled the terror to come.
Then, penny-eyed, that gentleman of wounds: then, dead and ready
  for burial, the wounded man
Old cock from nowheres and the heaven's egg: the ancient and self-
  born penis / that came before the question / about the chicken
  and the egg / born fatherless like the world / from the egg of
  Orpheus
With his bones unbuttoned to the half-way winds: standing cold and
  naked and dead / in the coat of his flesh / in the winds that blow /
  between birth and death
Hatched from the windy salvage on one leg: hatched from the
  wreckage of the storm and its rescue,
Scraped at my cradle in a walking word: told to my infant self all the
  terrors / of the world through which he now must wander
That night of time under the Christward shelter: with the darkness
  of *Deus Absconditus* filling it, and Christ at the end of it.
"I am the long world's gentleman, he said": "I am the world's long
  body" he told me, "contemporaneous with my aeon and
  stretched along its span—"
And share my bed with Capricorn and Cancer: "lying head and toes
  to the Poles, I am the still shaft of the turning cycle; I am with
  you through all days, till the Earth shall be no more."

This poem is so *hermetic* that the *hermeneutic* of it must give rise
to a second secret, nearly as convoluted as the first (but not quite).
But who exactly is this "Gentleman"? He is wounded; he is dead yet
living; he is perched like a heron on one leg on the "heron-priested
shore". It is as if he were—like the "Gentle Jesus" of Wesley's
hymn—*the ghost of Christ*, still perched on his one-legged cross: the
second corpse of Him that never rose from the dead nor ascended
into heaven, but remains to this day, Hell still unharried, in the
ground beneath us, and walks abroad at night, in the air all around
us—being, precisely, all that's left of the Divine Immanence in the
dark night of the soul, in the time of the death of God.

Now for logopoeia—and here's where we encounter a lot of people who seem to be very suspicious of *somebody with something to
say*. What is he, a propagandist, a preacher, an ad-man? A fanatic, a
terrorist, a seducer? Nobody is willing to *know* anything anymore.

"Don't even try and understand / Just find a place to make your stand" sang the Eagles back in the 70s. We tried all that *knowing* business in the 20th century and came up nothing but two world wars and the earth in ruins. Been there, done that—too much information—*I don't want to know.* (Where have you been for the past thirty years, man? Don't you know that *meaning is gauche?*)

Or let's tone it down a little and observe that there is still a certain degree of suspicion, in literary circles, of the *didactic* poem, like John Pope's "Essay on Man". Who is he to tell us what's what in the universe? He certainly doesn't pretend to be some "enthusiast" (as they called them in the 18th century), some visionary with a private revelation and looking to found a cult. But if he has no personal authority to teach us anything, where could his pretended authority have come from—slipped under his door in the dead of night—except from the *established* system of reality? There may actually be some substance to this suspicion of the poet's authority to teach, given the *ideological insanity* presently burning across the global landscape, and the tendency of poets to get diverted from the main road by various intellectual glamours. Nonetheless, there are some poets who really do know something, and consequently have something to say worth listening to. It was to shame the coward who wants to believe that nobody can actually know anything that Michael McClure wrote his "Hymn to St. Geryon, I" (see p. 180–181)—and to make sure that I never became a coward like that, Lew Welch once *impressed* upon me (as if stamping an image on a blank coin): "It's true *because I say so!*" Sometimes, if a man is faithful to his individual truth—not to his individual vanity or rationalization or self-interest—then God will back him up. The Almighty may make some changes in his vision—like a good editor will, to help him clarify his intent—but since He created each of us to be that one self and nobody else, He is not about to undo His work. He blesses those who become themselves, but He is equally ruthless with those who distort themselves and fall below themselves and betray themselves. "It's true because I say so" is madness if we think we can arbitrarily decree what is to be true when we can't even make the traffic signal change any faster than it normally would just because we want to get someplace in a hurry. The real meaning of "it's true because I say so" is: I've been given something that I *must say*, so there must be a for me reason to say it, a shame if I fail in my duty to say it, and a coming into exactly where I'm supposed to be if I say it right. And all of this just flows through me, and out of me, from something beyond me. Certainly it is *made*—the Greek word *poetes* means "maker"—but it is not *made up*.

A major modern English poem, in four parts, that relies heavily on logopoeia is T.S. Eliot's *Four Quartets*; in the section entitled "Burnt Norton" we encounter lines like this:

> Time present and time past
> Are both perhaps present in time future,
> And time future contained in time past.
> If all time is eternally present
> All time is unredeemable.

The statement is spare, compact, rhythmic, yet it is pretty thin on music, and totally devoid of image; it relies much more on *what* is said than on *how* it is said.

More melopoetic, because composed of rhyming couplets, and more phanopoetic because of the insects, birds and animals that fill it (reminding us in some ways of a medieval bestiary), though primarily logopoetic in form, is *Auguries of Innocence* by William Blake. Here is an excerpt:

> …The Bat that flits at close of Eve
> Has left the Brain that won't believe.
> The Owl that calls upon the Night
> Speaks the Unbeliever's fright.
> He who shall hurt the little Wren
> Shall never be belov'd by Men.
> He who the Ox to wrath has mov'd
> Shall never be by Woman lov'd.
> The wanton Boy that kills the Fly
> Shall feel the Spider's enmity.
> He who torments the Chafer's sprite
> Weaves a Bower in endless Night.
> The Catterpillar on the Leaf
> Repeats to thee thy Mother's grief.
> Kill not the Moth nor Butterfly,

For the Last Judgement draweth nigh.
He who shall train the Horse to War
Shall never pass the Polar Bar.
The Beggar's Dog & Widow's Cat,
Feed them & thou wilt grow fat.
The Gnat that sings his Summer's song
Poison gets from Slander's tongue.
The poison of the Snake & Newt
Is the sweat of Envy's Foot.
The poison of the Honey Bee
Is the Artist's Jealousy.
The Prince's Robes & Beggars' Rags
Are Toadstools on the Miser's Bags.
A truth that's told with bad intent
Beats all the Lies you can invent.
It is right it should be so;
Man was made for Joy & Woe;
And when this we rightly know
Thro' the World we safely go…

Another, probably more accessible example of poetry that relies primarily on logopoeia is "How to Give Yourself Away" by Lew Welch, a meditation on the allegory of Plato's Cave:

The cave of the mind is the
cave of the mind, and we
seek the opening,
the way out.

And the way out is simply that:
Out.

Compassion. The Flower.

The Flower of this, our Human being, is
Out.

The door of the cave.   Compassion.

We turn our backs to the blackened wall.

We do not want our recognizable shadows cast upon
the blackened wall.

We turn our backs to it.

We take the hand of our beloved and say:
"I cannot go it alone."

And our beloved will take our hand and we will
simply walk away. But it will mostly be done in
twos.

And this is not even "I and Thou."

It is simpler than that.

"Out of your Mind" means:
Not inside there burrowing about
For a change.

And lastly, this by Jack Gilbert, the first half of his poem "The
Great Fires":

Love is apart from all things.
Desire and excitement are nothing beside it.
It is not the body that finds love.
What leads us there is the body.
What is not love provokes it.
What is not love quenches it.
Love lays hold of everything we know.
The passions which are called love
also change everything to a newness
at first. Passion is clearly the path
but does not bring us to love.
It opens the castle of our spirit
so that we might find the love which is
a mystery hidden there.
Love is one of the many great fires...

And although the examples of logopoeia given above are all on
more-or-less exalted themes (in line with my own tastes), the definition of that word is still perfectly satisfied by Robert Frost's dry
and down-to-earth line, "Good fences make good neighbors".

In the greatest poetry, phanopoeia, melopoeia and logopoeia are perfectly balanced and mutually reinforcing. What we know with our "left brain" we also see with our "right brain"; both concept and image are driven deep into our consciousness by the shaped power of sound. This convergence of music, image and meaning is capable of producing some of the most powerful emotional experiences possible in the arts, experiences in which feeling does not distort, veil or dissipate understanding but rather shapes and expands it till it fills our whole being: body, soul and Spirit.

Perhaps the best example in English of the perfect balance and synthesis between phanopoeia, melopoeia and logopoeia is the poem "Byzantium" by William Butler Yeats.

3

More on the Muse

THE IDEA that a poet, especially a lyric poet, is inspired by the Muse is fairly passé at this point in time; if She is mentioned at all it is most likely in a jocular manner. A human being (usually female) who is thought to have inspired a male artist is sometimes called his Muse, in a more-or-less cavalier tone, but the idea is rarely taken seriously any more. One of the last poets to invoke Her on any level was perhaps Philip Lamantia, in his lines "Blue Grace behind dark glasses / Steps out of a hundred white cars all over town. . . ." Nor should we forget Lew Welch's humorous yet dead-serious warning, that "Anyone who confuses his mistress with his muse is asking for real trouble from both of them." Be that as it may, the Muse is a formidable reality that no amount of easy caricature can domesticate. She is much more than a literary conceit, a quaint explanation for how and why words may suddenly appear in our heads. She is more on the order of the *dakini* in Tibetan yoga, a subtle feminine presence who renders the contemplative labor of the yogi truly fertile in spiritual terms, so that it doesn't end up as a self-enclosed form of "mental masturbation".

Federico García Lorca, in his great essay "The Duende: Theory and Divertissement", [from the Grove Press edition of *The Poet in New York*, Ben Belitt's translation] defines three types of poetic inspiration: that by the Angel, that by the Muse, and that by the Duende:

> The Angel guides and endows, like Saint Raphael, or prohibits and avoids, like Saint Michael, or foretells, like Saint Gabriel. The Angel dazzles; but it flies over men's heads and remains in mid-air, shedding his grace; and the man, without any effort whatever, realizes his work, or his fellow-feeling, or his dance. The angel on

the road to Damascus, and he who entered the crevice of the little balcony of Assisi, or that other angel who followed in the footsteps of Heinrich Suso, *commanded*—and there was no resisting his radiance, for he waved wings of steel in an atmosphere of predestination.

The Muse dictates, and, in certain cases, prompts. There is relatively little she can do, for she keeps aloof and is so full of lassitude (I have seen her twice) that I myself have had to put half a heart of marble in her. The Poets of the Muse hear voices and do not know where they come from; but surely they are from the Muse, who encourages them and sometimes devours them entirely. [pp. 155-156]

But the Duende is something else. The name comes from *duen de la casa*, "Lord of the House", a sort of elf or household spirit in Spanish folklore—although, among Muslims, who ruled Andalusia for 800 years, "Lord of the House" is an epithet of Allah, "the House" being the Kaaba. Lorca says:

Manuel Torres, to my mind a man of exemplary blood culture, once issued this splendid phrase while listening to Falla himself play his "Nocturno del Generalife": "Whatever has black sounds has *duende*." There is no greater truth.

These "black sounds" are a mystery, the roots that probe through the mire we all know of, and do not understand, but which furnishes us with whatever is sustaining in art. Black sounds: so said the celebrated Spaniard, thereby concurring with Goethe, who, in effect, defined the *duende* when he said, speaking of Paganini: "A mysterious power that all may feel and no philosophy can explain."

The *duende*, then, is a power and not a construct, it is a struggle and not a concept. I have heard an old guitarist, a true virtuoso, remark, "The *duende* is not in the throat, the *duende* comes up from inside, up from the very soles of the feet." That is to say, it is not a question of aptitude, but of a true and viable style—of blood, in other words; of what is oldest in culture: of creation made act.

This "mysterious power that all may feel and no philosophy can explain" is, in sum, the earth-force, the same *duende* that fired the heart of Nietzsche, who sought it out in its external form on the

Rialto Bridge, or in the music of Bizet, without ever finding it, or understanding that the *duende* he pursued had rebounded from the mystery-minded Greeks to the dancers of Cádiz or the gored, Dionysian cry of Silvero's *siguiriya*. . . . [pp. 154–155]

The arrival of the *Duende* always presupposes a radical change in all the forms as they existed on the old plane. It gives a sense of refreshment unknown until then, together with that quality of the just-opening rose, of the miraculous, which comes and instils an almost religious transport. . . . [p. 158]

The *Duende* . . . will not approach at all if he does not see the possibility of death, if he is not convinced that he will circle death's house. . . . [p. 162]

Lorca's Angel, Muse and Duende are Spirit, Soul and Body—or rather Body instilled with Spirit. The Spirit contains everything and invokes everything and transforms everything, but when it appears in the guise of Lorca's Angel it has only just announced its presence; it has not yet come *down* to harrow our souls and our bodies so as to bring forth the flame and the diamond. As the Grace of God descends, it calls *up* that other face of God hidden in the flesh, the power the Hindus call the *kundalini*. The Soul speaking for herself, neither directly inspired by the Spirit nor intimately in love with the Body, is Lorca's Muse; her lassitude is her self-involvement, which may even indicate a vain and moody rejection of the Spirit Himself when He arrives—as if the Virgin Mary at the Annunciation, wishing to retain her youthful figure for as long as possible, had simply told the Angel Gabriel "no thank you". If she had made this refusal she could neither have brought forth the Word made Flesh nor functioned as the Muse for Dante Aligheri, through her delegated representatives St. Lucy and Beatrice Portinari, when he essayed to compose his great *Divine Comedy*. The Body, unless it remains a dense and unresponsive boulder, pelted by rain and whacked by hail-stones, is what will give birth to the Duende, the full and passionate response of both Body and Soul to the Spirit's advent. If this were not its role then why would we poets, exalted spiritual idealists that we are (the irony is deliberate here) elect to retain the "vile bodies" that chain us to this bourgeois, Philistine world? The Duende is the *Shakti*, and consequently—according to my own terminology—

29

she represents the Muse in her fullest and most powerful form. The Angel announces the Incarnation; the Duende is the Cross, the Tomb and the Resurrection. Francis of Assisi could have never received his *stigmata*—Lorca—except through the Duende.

We carry the seed of the Divine Word within us—but if that seed finds no fertile ground to fall to, and rot inside of, and be reborn from the embrace of, it will simply return to the transcendent world it came from, having found no soul and no body in this lower world capable of *listening with all they are.* The Muse hears that Word as soon as God speaks It, conceives of It inside her, then commands us to repeat It in mortal space and time, or as much of It as our sensitivity and stamina and capacity and willingness to sacrifice our identifications and obscurities makes possible for us to contain. But if the Muse simply draws that Word out of us without our active participation, if not against our will—or whatever fragment of the Divine Word she senses sleeping inside us—then she is the devouring Muse of Lorca, the Substantial Pole in rebellion against the Essential Pole that we have failed to realize and take responsibility for, the castrating Kali. But if, in obedience to the Spirit within us and thus acting as Its delegated *kalifa* in the realm of language, we take full responsibility for what we *mean to say*, then She is the Wife of the Word that rises up inside us to meet Her—in precisely the same sense, though in a much more limited domain, that the Virgin Mary was the Spouse of the Holy Spirit. As Mary said "my soul doth magnify the Lord", so the Muse is the mirror in which the Divine Word appears to us, fully formed and resonant with power, in this lower world almost too poor to contain it without bursting at the seams. It was this vision of the Muse as *Shakti* that led Gary Snyder to write, in his poem "Regarding Wave":

> The Voice
> is a Wife
> to
>
>
> him still.

Manifestation is based on polarity, consequently the outer manifestation of hidden things that we call poetry must arise from the polarity between Speaker and Listener, two poles that sometimes change places: either we speak into the listening Silence, or that Silence itself suddenly speaks to us, transforming us into the listeners. In any case, it is the function of the Muse to prevent us from falling into the sort of narcissistic subjectivity that is always the death of poetry; she is there to make sure we aren't just talking to ourselves. In the traditional ballad of "Thomas Rymer" from the Child collection ("rymer" means "poet"), True Thomas is abducted by the Queen of Faerie—clearly a Pagan British rendition of the poet's Muse—who conducts him through various chambers of the underworld, and lays upon him the taboo that, while a guest in Her realm, he must speak to Her and no-one else. If the poet obeys this condition—if he knows how to become quiet enough to *hear Her listening*—then his aim and his words will be true.

⁓ 4 ⁓
Mythopoesis

MYTHOPOESIS, in Greek, means "myth-making"; a myth is *a story that is always true*. Mythopoetic writing, whether in verse or prose, has traveled so far into the world of metaphor and symbol that it has ended by producing a narrative that no longer necessarily seems metaphorical or symbolic at all, but rather presents itself as if it were the "literal reality" of another world—the sort of imaginary world that most contemporary readers assume the writer has simply invented because it intrigued him, in hopes that it would also intrigue us. J. R. R. Tolkien was fascinated by the idea of Mordor and magicians, of Elves and Orcs, so he wrote his *Lord of the Rings* trilogy to share his fascination with us, and hopefully make some money.

However, it is impossible to move that far into the world of metaphor and symbol without encountering metaphysics. Metaphysical realities can be expressed (partially at least) in the sort of discursive prose used by philosophers and theologians, yet metaphysics can never be entirely divorced from mythopoesis. Spiritual principles and mystical states of consciousness are notoriously ineffable; anyone who tries to render them in matter-of-fact prose will encounter the inescapable limitations of any language that tries to express the realities that lie beyond words. And that fact is that *all* realities lie beyond words; any translation into human language of our experience of an 18-wheeler truck whipping past us at close range as we sit in our parked car by the side of the road will encounter the same inevitable limitations that the mystic runs into when trying to render—in mere words—the eternity, the flawlessness and the authority of the naked presence of God. Maybe the very fact that *every* experience is greater than our description of it (to others or to ourselves)—perhaps infinitely greater—should be numbered among the classic proofs of the existence of God, like Kant's *noumenon* or "thing-in-itself", which is unknowable in terms of anything other than itself. Nonetheless, language (and music, and the plastic arts) has other resources than discursive prose to render the Ineffable: the *phanopoeia* (image-making power) and *melopoeia* (music-making power) of poetry, as well as the tools of symbolism and metaphor that both poetry and mythopoesis (in either verse or prose) can draw upon to supplement, though certainly not negate, the rationality and logic of the philosopher and the scriptural exegesis of the theologian.

On one level at least, it is true to say that metaphysics is the exegesis of mythopoesis, just as mythopoesis is the *incarnation* of metaphysics—though metaphysical truth can also be incarnated and expressed through music, dance, song, painting, sculpture and the other arts. Mythopoetic verse can transmit metaphysical truth to all the levels and systems of the brain, "higher" and "lower", that are affected by music and rhythm, mental visualization, and declarative statement; it simultaneously affects our emotions, our memory, our rational faculties, and our motor functions. And in terms of visual imagery alone, it is undoubtedly true that displaying the dramatic actions of a god or hero or magic animal to the human imagination, a figure that is also recognized as symbolizing something higher, affects more brain-systems than the simple contemplation of a static image—though such static contemplation, as in the case of the traditional Hindu or Buddhist *mandala* for example, can lead our consciousness to some pretty deep spaces on its own. And when a poem is both sung and danced, like poems used to be before the Daughters of Memory got caught up in their sibling rivalry, these effects are greatly enhanced. It is no wonder, then, that the need to express in outer terms, insofar as is possible, the inner reality of the *Mysterium Tremendum*, would lead poets, liturgists and theurgists to synthesize a number of the arts, so as to render as closely as possible the supremely synthetic realizations that metaphysical contemplation provides. However, since there are certain dimensions of our rational faculty, and of the brain-areas associated with it, that are left out of the picture by poetry and mythopoesis—

33

the aspects that, after we distance ourselves from a particular experience, begin to ask, "but what did it all *mean*?"—the philosophical exegesis of mythopoesis is also an integral aspect of metaphysics. *Mythos* must be supplemented by *logos*, otherwise it will sink to the level of recreational fantasy or propaganda. And the fact is, the same truth can be told in either language. When St. Thomas Aquinas informs us that "In the case of God, Essence and Being are One", he is saying the same thing that Yah-weh says in the Book of Exodus when, after Moses asks Him His Name, He answers from the Burning Bush, "I Am That I Am". *Mythos*, a symbolically dense form of expression, can transmit more metaphysical truth per cubic centimeter than *logos* can, yet *logos* is indispensable for its ability to shine a mental, intellective light on the existential reality of *mythos*. If we don't know (like Dante did) that the centaur symbolizes the human personality driven and dominated by the passions, then we don't mentally understand it, but if we're incapable of visualizing the passion-dominated personality as a centaur, or some equally apt symbol, then we've never fully encountered it. This is why dreams, based as they are largely on the language of symbolic images, are necessary to supplement and expand our conscious understanding of a given situation. To the bare "facts" of that situation, dream-actions and dream-images add emotional nuance, unsuspected additional dimensions, and wider and subtler context.

In light of this we can see just how important a familiarity with the mythopoetic literature of the world is to our understanding of ourselves and the universe we live in. Just as it is doubly difficult for someone who lacks skill in dream recall and interpretation to reach integral self-knowledge (nor can anyone who is ignorant of mythopoesis really interpret dreams), so the one who is unfamiliar with world mythology and the functional nature of mythopoesis in human consciousness can neither fully grasp metaphysics nor adequately understand the workings of his or her own mind. Thus the study of myth and poetry provides much more than aesthetic enjoyment or cultural refinement; it lets us know ourselves and the world around us, as well as the invisible dimensions from which they spring, as a unified whole.

~~5~~

Nirukta and *Mantram*:
The Atemporal Morphology
of Language

JOHN CAREY, in his article "Etymology and Time" [*Temenos Academy Review* 5, Autumn 2002] in which he reaches some of the same conclusions I reached in the course of composing the present essay, points out that to say "*I* and *eye* are the same word" in etymological terms is simply wrong. They have totally different histories. They are no more identical, he says, than the word *God* and the word *guard* when pronounced with a Yankee accent.

But the Hindu linguistic science of *nirukta* is not etymology, at least in the historical sense; as Ananda Coomaraswamy points out in his essay on this subject ["Nirukta=Hermeneia" from *Coomaraswamy, Selected Papers, 2: Metaphysics*; Bollingen Series LXXXIX], it is a mode of *hermeneia*, the science of discerning the eternal or vertical causality, or correspondence, that links different levels of being. It is based on morphology rather than derivation; it is more like crystallography than historical analysis. To mistake *nirukta* for etymology is clearly an error. The act of tracing etymological derivations may open up new fields for the exercise of *nirukta*, but the fact remains that *nirukta* is vertical and eternal (or rather *aeonian*), while etymology is horizontal and temporal. *Nirukta* is the warp, etymology the weft, of the fabric of language.

Eternal does not mean *everlasting*: eternity doesn't *last*. And if it seems to last, it is not on the basis of temporal duration (Blake's "Memory"), but on the basis of an unbroken connection with its archetype (Blake's "Inspiration"). In temporal terms, a vertical correspondence or consonance between ontological levels may last the whole life of a spiritual civilization based on a Divine revelation, or it may last for only an instant. Here, from the poetry of Hafiz (translated by H. Wilberforce Clarke, "trans-created" by myself) is an example of a momentary sympathetic vibration in the vertical dimension, the *Axis Mundi*:

> When I knew that the Full Moon had paid with his living soul
>   for those pearls of Hafiz,
> At that very moment the sharp twang of the lute
> Touched the ear of Zuhra!

The occasion is as follows: A *sama* or spiritual concert is being performed in the presence of a Sufi shaykh. A poem of Hafiz, set to music, is being sung by the singing-girl Zuhra, probably to the accompaniment of a Persian *setar*. Hafiz is present, watching the shaykh like a hawk for any sign of his approval. Suddenly he sees that the shaykh has been moved to his depths; the song of Hafiz is like an arrow through his heart. And in the same eternal spiritual moment (*waqt*), the swell of the music and the singing of Zuhra reach a degree of transcendental perfection, inseparable from the spiritual state (*hal*) of the shaykh—and from Hafiz as witness of it. The perfection of the music has not caused the perfection of the singing, nor vice versa, nor has either one caused the state of the shaykh, nor has the state of the shaykh caused the musical/poetic epiphany, any more than the witnessing by Hafiz caused any of it: the moment, the *hal*, the *waqt* has descended, vertically and at once, upon all of them, from God; in Quranic terms, it has appeared simultaneously on the *horizons* and in their *souls*. The moment is eternal; it's over in a flash.

In the same way, meanings, and their verbal reflections, collect around archetypal Ideas, like bees returning to their hive. They are not *reincarnated,* horizontally, from the past, but *incarnated,* vertically, from Eternity, as Jesus declared Himself to be when he said: "Before Abraham came to be, I Am." Existing in synthetic mode on their plane of origin, they are analyzed or refracted as they enter earth-bound and time-conditioned human consciousness.

I and *eye*, etymologically speaking, are obviously not the same words. They have different histories, and the "pun" that connects

36

them, as John Carey points out, is possible only in relatively recent English, later than Chaucer. When we move to Spanish, it disappears: *Yo* is not a homophone for *ojo*. Yet the fact of their homophonic consonance, which is also a symbolic or poetic consonance, is not meaningless; it is significant.

Nirukta, as I see it, has two principles, which represent the extremes of its spectrum:

(1) As intelligible meanings collect around archetypal ideas—or as archetypal ideas are refracted into intelligible meanings—so those meanings draw to themselves, and are reflected as, words which exhibit morphological similarities that have no necessary etymological basis. Not all homophones or near-homophones are participants in the same Idea, yet it is undeniable that collections of homophones or near-homophones that do participate in a common Idea really exist; and this is relatively easy to demonstrate.

(2) Vowels, consonants and the words composed of them have specific *physiological resonances* of different qualities, experienced as resonating in different parts of the human body. And given that specific sounds stimulate specific areas or processes within the subtle nervous system, they constitute, in the form of "seed-syllables," the physiological analogues of archetypal Ideas, this being the basis of the science of *mantram*. Thus *nirukta* could be defined as the practice of "hearing all sounds as *mantram*" in the realm of human language.

In Arabic, based as it is on (usually) tri-literal consonantal roots, all the words derived from the same root possess a *metaphorical convergence of meanings* that is often complex and subtle, but always ultimately intelligible. Consequently, certain poetic effects are possible in Arabic that English cannot manage, or that it can only approach via techniques such as *punning*, which is not appropriate (in most cases) for expressing any degree of subtlety or sublimity—though as we will see at the end of the essay, this limitation does not always apply. English, however, though it is devoid of true consonantal roots, does possess what might be termed "quasi-roots" that obey some of the same principles as true roots. The quasi-root "PK", for example, represents a fairly obvious cluster of meanings relating to an archetypal idea. *Pick, pike, peck, poke, peak* all have to do with something that comes to a point (German *punkt*). Most of these words are etymologically related, but they also share the same quality of physiological resonance. The sound *P* is made by an explosive expression of air past the lips, which in terms of psycho-physiological resonance denotes "expression made against resistance by means of breath gathered to a point", where "breath" = "the totality of potential or undifferentiated meaning which is life itself, before it is broken up into words." The sound *K*, on the other hand, represents an almost complete stoppage of breath at the palate. Therefore the root "PK" denotes "the abrupt stoppage of pointed expression at a limit or barrier." To *pick* is to strike a flat surface, such as the ground or a block of ice, with a pointed object, but it is also to *choose*. When our consciousness comes to a point, a point which strikes against the flat surface of undifferentiated meaning, unparticularized perception, or dull incomprehension, one specific meaning is *picked out* from its surroundings. (And one reason that climbing a *peak* represents spiritual development is that, at the summit, the whole bulk of the mountain comes to a *point* in the face of the undifferentiated sky—just as, in meditation, consciousness must become one-pointed in the face of a Reality that is empty of specific determinations.)

The English quasi-root "SP" also relates to expression, but in this case an energetic flow or process beginning in the invisible world, denoted by *S*, comes to expression, via *P*, then it explosively crosses the barrier between the hidden or the undifferentiated and the manifest or particular, or between shapeless flowing energy and concrete form. Most "SP" words have to do with expression, manifestation, projection or extension, whether or not they are etymologically related (and not all of them are): *Spit, spew, spurt, spark, span, spar, speed, spur, spear, speak, spell,* etc. All of these are aspects or actions of the *Spirit*, the creative Breath of God. In the words of Psalm 104, "Send forth Thy Spirit and they shall be created, and Thou shalt renew the face of the earth." The speech of the Creator, like the light of the sun, radiates in all directions, like the *spokes* of a wheel.

This verbal clustering of meanings also happens in the world of dreams, as anyone who has made a study of dreams and dream analysis will have learned. For example, I once dreamt of a being named "Eagleaxis" who carried me from earth up to the heavens, depositing me in a twilight ampitheatre where I met my dead father. Since my flight was vertical, the "axis" in the name indicated the *Axis Mundi*; the "eagle" element in the name was the power to soar high, high up that axis. And the "galaxis" element was another rendition of the *Axis Mundi*, since the Milky Way Galaxy (*galaxy* itself is derived from the Greek word for "milky") was seen by many primitive peoples as the road traveled by the souls of the departed to the next world: the *Axis Mundi* precisely. In other words, there is a stratum of the human mind, considered to be part of the "unconscious" by those who are not conscious of it, that understands and composes linguistic forms according to the laws of *nirukta*; James Joyce's *Finnegan's Wake* is the great western example of this type of composition. On that level of being, words are not differentiated so as to indicate (among other things) discrete sense-objects, but rather synthesized in order to point, as if by triangulation, toward specific transcendental Ideas. When William Blake heard, in poetic dictation, the names of the "Zoas", Urizen and Urthona, which appear in his Prophetic Books *The Four Zoas*, *Milton*, and *Jerusalem*, he was tapping that stratum of the mind. S. Foster Damon in *A Blake Dictionary* speculates that Urizen, Zoa of the South, of the element Air and the rational mind, is a pun on both "horizon" and "your reason," and that Urthona, Zoa of the North, of the element Earth and the Prophetic Imagination, is a pun on "earth owner" (and I hear in it also an echo of "throne"). In "The Marriage of Heaven and Hell", Blake defines *reason* as "the bound or outward circumference of Energy", i.e., its *horizon*, while the Zoa Urthona, who "owns the earth", would of course also be *enthroned* upon it. Here, since we are dealing with newly-coined names where the question of etymological antecedents hardly enters the question, we can see how a certain faculty of the human mind spontaneously combines words or syllables from many sources, either consciously or unconsciously (remembering that it *is* possible at the same time to be both conscious and spontaneous), so as to produce unique linguistic constructions designed to suggest multiple meanings in synthetic mode—in other words, Platonic Ideas. We have every reason to suppose that such a faculty has been an integral aspect of human consciousness since its beginnings, particularly since it can apparently operate in the dream-state; and if this is so, then it is co-extensive with human language, and has always influenced it.

In Hindu Yoga, the mantric syllable AUM is designed to collect all the parts or fragments of consciousness and return them to their primal Unity. (These fragments of consciousness, or rather the processes that produce this fragmentation, are physiologically represented by habitual tensions or knots in the psycho-physical nervous system, each knot expressing itself as a complex of unconscious, obsessive sub-vocal speech and the specific, reactive emotions related to it, as well as to the specific, limited worldview arising from the complex in question.) *AAAA* collects all the elements of waking consciousness, merging them into *UUUU*—dream or imaginal consciousness—which is in turn merged into *MMMM*, dreamless sleep or deep trance, which ultimately dissolves into the silence which is *turiya*, the fourth or supreme state of consciousness, the undifferentiated Matrix or Witness of all the others. However, this mantric quality of language may also be effective in bringing consciousness *out* of the original Unity into clear differentiation and expression—a motion that is not ultimately opposed to Unity, since to be conscious of differentiation (we are usually relatively unconscious of it because we are enmeshed in it) is to posit Unity, given that differentiation can only be contemplated as it really is from the standpoint of Unity. (When your consciousness is foggy and diffuse, and you need to make it more *punctilious*, try using the "PK" root as a mantra; when your expression is blocked and bottled up, try using "SP". Then let me know what happens.) The process whereby Unity posits multiplicity is rendered in the Qur'an by the verse *And Our word unto a thing, when We intend it, is only that We say unto it: Be! and it is* (Q.16:40). Mantrically considered, the Arabic word for "be", *kun*, renders a buildup of energy in the *batin*, the Unseen—anatomically speaking, at the point where the back of the tongue locks against the palate—followed by an explosive release of this energy, in subtle form, into the *zahir*, the visible, outer world.

In view both of the mantric dimension of language perceived in terms of specific physiological resonances, and of the fact that morphologically similar words gather around archetypal Ideas like moths around a candle, we can return to the coincidence of *I* and *eye*, and see something new in it. Both Islamic Sufism and Eastern Orthodox Christian Hesychasm symbolize the indwelling Transcendental Intellect—*Nous* in Greek, *Ruh* in Arabic—as "the Eye of the Heart"—a name which in Hindu terms is immediately recognizable as the Absolute Witness or *Atman*, which is said to reside in the *hrdayam*, the Cave of the Heart, and which is commonly symbolized by an "Eye" which cannot see itself as an object. This *Atman* is realized, in *jñana-yoga* as taught by Sri Ramana Maharshi, as representing the ultimate "answer" to the question "Who am I?" Thus the Eye of the Heart is strictly analogous to, or another name for, the "I" *residing* in the Heart—to that reality Meister Eckhart indicated when he declared, "My truest 'I' is God."

But if "the Eye of the Heart" is also "the 'I' in the Heart", what accounts for the "pun" in which "I" and "Eye" become the same English sound, given that they are totally unrelated etymologically, and that their coincidence of meaning pertains mostly to the level of the *Imago Dei*, the *Atman*, the essential Self? Is it a "mere coincidence", or is there more to it?

I believe that there is more to it. In English we say that "the eye is the window of the soul"—the *soul* being the true or essential "I"; the curse "damn your eyes" is essentially another way of saying "damn your soul." So "I" and "eye" were analogous as concepts in English *before* they were homophonous—and it may well be that their conceptual affinity was the *source* of that homophony, the very thing that ultimately drew them together, after long ages, into a single English sound. Can we prove this? Probably not. But we can certainly demonstrate the existence, in any language, of homophony or near-homophony as reflective of conceptual analogy, outside of any demonstrable etymological affinity. Just look for it and you will find it everywhere. It's not contrived or made up; it's really out there in the topography of language, ready and waiting to be discovered— and I submit that anyone who can't see it has been laboriously *taught* not to see, or hear, what is right there before his or her eyes and ears—as most of us certainly have been taught in our time. This sort of atrophy of what once was undoubtedly a common human faculty, based on an ideological restriction of consciousness to a narrow set of received ideas, is part and parcel of the loss of poetic or symbolic or metaphysical consciousness in the modern world, which in turn is inseparable from the tyranny of the materialistic, historical outlook. We are forced by our education, and by all the material processes of modern material life, to see things only in their becoming, not in their being; to understand a great deal about how they work or where they come from, but less and less about what they *are*. To see things as they are, in this sense, is to see them as symbols, not mere material results; it is to see them not historically but *sub specie aeternitatis*. And the faculty by which things can be seen in this manner is, precisely, the Eye of the Heart. The Eye of the Heart does not see things as measurable material or quasi-material objects, but as Seers in their own right—as instances of the One Self of All—as *I*'s capable not only of being looked at, but also (as it were) of looking back. As with a human beloved, the measurable attributes of something seen in this way are negligible; all that really matters is that thing's *uniqueness*; this is what Blake meant when he said that Divine Reality does not manifest as abstract categories but as "minute particulars." Things are witnessed in this way by virtue of what the Buddhists call *tathata*, "suchness". A Russian Orthodox Christian, Vladimir Maximov, in *The Seven Days of Creation*, describes his vision of *tathata*, of minute particulars, in these terms: "it is as if I were seeing the forest for the first time. A fir tree was not only a fir tree but something else much greater. The dew on the grass was not just dew in general. Each drop existed on its own. *I could have given a name to every puddle on the road.*" These are the words of a man who, for one brief moment when, for him, Eternity descended into time, learned how to read the world like a book. And if it is possible to read the world like a book, it should certainly also be possible to read *language* like a book.

Mantrically speaking, the word "I" or "eye"—"AI"—is a seed-syllable of recollection. The sound *AAAA* resonates in the throat and projects so fully from the throat into the outer world that we can hardly feel it anywhere else in the body; it thus relates us to the world of named, defined and interrelated objects we know as the waking world. [NOTE: This is true of the *A* preceded by a glottal stop, as in English and Arabic; the various *A* sounds of Sanskrit resonate more deeply in the chest, as in the word *aham*, "I am".] The sound *IIII* (the long "e") resonates in the palate, a resonance that extends from there to (among other destinations) the *añja-chakra* or "third eye." The motion of the sound "AI" from the world back into the self allows it to be *physiologically symbolic* of a particular range of meanings. As "eye" it represents the gathering of the sense-world into the self, as with the sense of sight. As "I" it represents the recognition of the world as a reflection or *Shakti* of the Self (what Blake called our "Emanation"); in terms of the Spanish cry "*ay!*," it expresses an identification with the world that is suddenly brought up short by the realization of every person's essential solitude—*soledad*—and consequently functions as a lament.

If we confuse *niukta* and its sister science of *mantram* with historical etymology, then we are clearly in error. But if we imagine that etymology is the only possible approach to the meanings of words, we are equally in error. *Nirukta* is often characterized as "folk etymology", considered to be based on spurious uninformed speculation by persons ignorant of etymology and linguistics; and folk etymology is indeed spurious when it claims the power to take the place and do the work of etymology proper. When recognized as an instance of "folk metaphysics," however, a collective intuition of the Platonic Ideas—if not of a profoundly conscious understanding of the symbolic dimension of all manifest forms verbally rendered by certain highly-trained and fully-informed individuals, then implanted in the "folk memory" for safe-keeping—it makes up an essential and irreplaceable aspect of contemplative aesthetics, without which both the natural world and the world of sacred art would be opaque to us, devoid of any intrinsic significance. To Primordial Man, however, as to any well-informed participant in one of the great Divine Revelations, both the natural world and the landscape of language are intrinsically significant; not only that, but their orders of significance are both analogous and complementary, which is why both the primal human being and the religious believer, if true to their respective archetypes, possess the ability to read the world like a book, and to enter a sacred Book and walk around in it, as if it were a world. In the words of St. Maximos the Confessor,

[The Logos], while hiding himself for our benefit in a mysterious way, in the *logoi*, shows himself to our minds to the extent of our ability to understand, through visible objects which act like letters of the alphabet, whole and complete both individually and when related together.

And according to the Holy Qur'an:

In your creation and in all the beasts scattered on the earth there are signs for people of true faith. In the alternation of night and day, and in the provision which Allah sendeth down from the heavens whereby he quickeneth the earth after its death, and in the distribution of the winds, are signs for people who are intelligent (Q.45:4–6).

It is this sort of apprehension of the meanings intrinsic to both language and the natural world that allowed one of the greatest American poets of nature, the Buddhist Gary Snyder, to write, in his book *Regarding Wave*:

The Voice
is a Wife
to

him still.

"Wife" is cognate with "wave", and "vibrate", as both are with the German *weib*, "woman"—and "still", here, means both "even now", and "motionless." "Him still" is the impassive Witness, the *Shakti-man*, the "Power-holder", the vertical *warp* of the fabric of language; the horizontal Voice is the *woof* or *weft* of it, the *Shakti*, the Power herself. The eternal goddess Athena, feminine Logos of the ancient Greeks—whose Hindu form is Gayatri, goddess of the mother-*mantram* of the Vedic universe—sits at the loom of language, forever *weaving* it, before the motionless Eye of the Heart.

VAC!

✎ 6 ✎

Homer, Poet of *Maya*

A slightly shorter version of this essay appeared in my book *Know-ings, in the Arts of Metaphysics, Cosmology and the Spiritual Path*, Sophia Perennis, 2008

IN HIS great epics the *Iliad* and the *Odyssey*, Homer expresses a complete doctrine of *Maya*, and of the cycle of Divine manifestation as unfolded and dissolved by *Maya*. Taken together, the two poems constitute a mythopoetic *cycle* in the strict sense of that term: the story of the creation and destruction of the universe (a word that means "one turn")—which, in sober fact, is the only story there is.

According to the Hindus, *Maya* is the Great Mother of manifest existence; She is the creative illusion or magical apparition of Brahman, the Formless Absolute, in terms of the finite field of forms. *Maya* is not strictly unreal or non-existent; it's simply that She is not what She seems; to use the traditional Hindu simile, She is like "a rope mistaken for a snake." *Maya* appears in two forms: *avidya-maya* or "ignorance-apparition", and *vidya-maya* or "wisdom-appa-rition." Since *Maya* is not what She seems, she seduces us to try and make sense of Her, a task which is both inescapable and ultimately impossible. As *avidya-maya* she lures us into a false identification of Absolute Reality with the relative world, and in so doing creates that world; as *vidya-maya*, she lures us (as in Plato's *Symposium*) toward identification with ever higher and more comprehensive images of Absolute Reality, each of which is progressively discarded in favor of a greater conception, until all images and conceptions are finally transcended and Absolute Reality realized.

The *Iliad* is the epic of *avidya-maya*, the *Odyssey* the epic of *vidya-maya*. Helen, the cause for an expansive, imperialistic war, the "face that launched a thousand ships", is *avidya-maya*, the power that

45

lures men into worldly identification, conflict and dissipation. Pene-lope, the wife of Odysseus "the cunning", the image of retreat, of withdrawal from the world, of home, is *vidya-maya*. She is the power of recollection, of return to the "center in the midst of condi-tions"; she is Holy Wisdom. In the epics of Homer, Troy is the City of This World, and Ithaca is the City of God. And Athene, the weaver-goddess who transcends the action of the epics but whose power is immanent everywhere within them, is *Mahamaya* herself.

The end of the expansive and dissipative attempt to "conquer the world", to control material conditions, to possess and dominate the "ten-thousand things" is, precisely, *apocalypse*—the end of the world—the burning of Troy. And Odysseus knew this. Like any wise and cunning man, he knew that the war to conquer the world would end in destruction and nothing else, that Troy would burn, that the victorious Agamemnon would be murdered—and that Helen, once "rescued," would simply become irrelevant. And so, of course, he tried to avoid the conflict; he flinched at the call to be born into this relative and conditioned world. Like many "draft dodgers" in the Vietnam War, he feigned madness to avoid service; he tried to plough a field with his plough harnessed to an ox and an ass, expressing the inevitable divergence of intent and division of the will that this world is made of, due to the fragmentation of the original human character (as the giant Ymir in Norse myth, and the Hindu Purusha, were dismembered to create the universe). But when his son was placed in front of the plough, he turned it aside—proving that he was not mad enough to destroy his own spiritual center and destiny. And so he had to go to war. He was wise enough to foresee the inevitable tragedy of the fall into this world of division, conflict and destruction—but *Maya*, the deceiver, was wiser than he. Only She knew the darkest secret of existence: that the descent into this world is really a *felix culpa*, a "fortunate sin"; that in the depth of the Great Mystery, the loss of God—felt and fought against and suffered through and finally redeemed—is in fact the deepest realization of God, that after "My God, my God, why hast Thou forsaken me?" comes "Into Thy hands I commend my spirit; it is finished."

Helen, in the *Iliad*, is shown sitting in Priam's palace in Troy, weaving a "double purple cloak" upon which appear the scenes of the great war between the Trojans and the Achaeans that she herself precipitated; by this she is revealed precisely as *avidya-maya*, who weaves the pattern of manifest existence, based as it is on *double-ness*, on division and polarity, like sexual reproduction; the world of visible manifestation is the world of the *dvandvas*, the pairs-of-opposites. But Penelope, Odysseus' wife, is also a weaver. She has told her many suitors that she will wed one of them when the shroud she is weaving, the shroud of her father-in-law Laertes, is finished—but every night, in order to put them off, she unweaves what she had woven during the day. Laertes, father of Odysseus, is his Principle and Origin, the aspect of God that pertains most directly to him, his archetype *in divinis*. And this world, to the wise, is not a cloak of the living, a purple garment fit for kings, depicting glorious and heroic struggles, but, precisely, the shroud of God, the veil that covers Him in death. This world unfolds in all its convincing multiplicity only when God is dead to us; only then, under the influence of *avidya-maya*, do we mistake this perishing world for Reality itself. Helen weaves the cloak of the world-illusion, but only Penelope shows it for what it is. Only *vidya-maya* can reveal to us the secret of *Maya* per se, that the pattern of existence woven on the Day of Brahman is unwoven again in the Night of Brahman, that the world created by *Maya* is not a stable reality, but a coming and going, a wheel of birth and death, an outbreathing and inbreathing of the Great Sleeper who dreams the universe.

The course of *vidya-maya* embraces the many journeys and battles and awakenings and realizations that are the spiritual Path; the *Odyssey*, the epic that depicts the struggles of Odysseus to be reunited with Penelope, with Holy Wisdom (under the guidance of the goddess Athene, the providential manifestation of that Wisdom, and Hermes her emissary), is the story of that Path. The stations of Odysseus' spiritual journey, symbolized by his long return from Troy to Ithaca, are as follows:

(1) The raid carried out by Odysseus and his men on the Cicones of Ismarus, in which the Greeks are defeated. This symbolizes the defeat of worldly ambitions, the proof that this world no longer holds anything of value for those who have embarked upon the spiritual Path.

(2) The land of the Lotus Eaters. This station, under the metaphor of drug addiction (possibly to opium) symbolizes the over-
coming of the World Trance, the nearly universal addiction of the
human race to the sort of worldly experience that denies any possibility of spiritual experience—either that or the habit of unconsciously translating the dawn of true spiritual experience back into
a different kind of worldly experience, notably the intoxicating
complacency represented by the Buddhists as *Deva-Loka*, the realm
of the long-lived gods where "ignorance is bliss". In terms of the
spiritual Path, Vajrayana practitioners are warned not to fall into
"the beautiful Hinayana peace", into the complacent illusion that
Enlightenment has already been achieved; by this they are chal-
lenged to overcome the curse of the lotus-eaters.

(3) The Island of the shepherd Polyphemus, the one-eyed
Cyclops, who devours several of Odysseus' men. Jesus said, "if thine
eye become single, thy whole body will be filled with light";
Polyphemus represents the dawning of this truth, the truth of the
Absolute One, on too low a level, resulting in the "absolutizing of
the relative", the precise error that creates religious fanatics, and
then devours them. The premature identification with the Transcendent One at the expense of Its multiple manifestation results
only in destruction; the rigor of Transcendence can be safely
encountered only after the soul has been unified in submission to
God's will. Before that time, the Eye of the One—like the "third eye"
of Shiva, the opening of which destroys the world illusion—must be
blinded, veiled; otherwise it will burn up all the traveler's spiritual
potential instead of putting it to effective use. Furthermore, to contemplate Unity at the level of the *head* can never be complete; Unity
can be realized in a stable way only at the level of the *heart*. However,
what appears to be only a disaster is in fact the secret beginning of
that necessary unification of soul. Throughout the *Odyssey*, Odysseus' followers are gradually killed off, until only he remains alive;
this symbolizes the process of *recollection*, the mortification of the
various divergent impulses of the soul, in terms of the affections, the
will and the thinking mind, until all that remains is unity of character and one-pointedness of spiritual attention and intent. As it says
in the *Tao Te Ching*, "Knowledge is gained by daily increment; the

Way is gained by daily loss—loss upon loss, until at last comes rest."

The name "Polyphemus" means "many-voiced"; what might be the symbolic meaning of a figure with many voices but only one eye? In terms of the contemplative act—one of whose sites, in Hindu *kundalini-* or *raja-yoga*, is the "third eye", the *ajña-chakra* in the center of the forehead—the Eye of God is One; according to Meister Eckhart, "the Eye through which I see God and the Eye through which He sees me are the same Eye"—which is to say that, in contemplation, the knower is one with the thing known. However, the *reflection* of this contemplative Unity on the mental level (whose yogic site is the *visshudha-chakra* situated at the throat) is multiple, like the image of the Sun reflected in the waves of the sea. We may be granted—or we may *steal*—a glimpse of spiritual Unity, but if we have not paid the price required for the full and stable realization of that Unity, this incandescent glimpse will immediately fall to the level of discursive thought with its many voices; consequently the mental substance will become over-energized, driving us to the obsessive and futile attempt—all-too-clearly in evidence in today's world—to *think every possible thought*. This is what it means to be "devoured by Polyphemus".

(4) Aeolus, the god of the winds, gives Odysseus a bag containing all the winds of the world, so that he will always have a fair wind in his voyage back to Ithaca. But his followers, out of curiosity, open the bag while Odysseus is asleep, let the winds loose, and all their ships are blown off course, back to their starting-point. This represents a wrong relationship to Divine Providence, based on lack of trust in God. If we dig up the seed every day to see if it is growing, the plant will never mature; if we arrogate to ourselves the right to see into the mind and Spirit of God, so as to better understand all the ramifications of our spiritual destiny—as if we could be better guardians and administrators of that destiny than God Himself— then we will be blown far off course. While Wisdom sleeps, curiosity wakes up and starts looking around; in the words of Frithjof Schuon, "mental passion pursuing intellectual intuition is like a wind that blows out the light of a candle."

(5) Landing on the Island of the Laestrygones, who are cannibals, Odysseus' men encounter a young girl, daughter of the king of the

49

island, who invites them to her father's court, where many are devoured. The princess symbolizes *avidya-maya*, who lures men to eat themselves up in worldly pursuits; spiritual curiosity ultimately results in a regression into worldliness. Nonetheless, the great purification continues. Cannibals are "self-eaters"; under the hidden influence of the Spirit, the divergent tendencies of the soul begin to destroy themselves by their own folly. As William Blake said, "If the fool would persist in his folly he would become wise."

(6) Next Odysseus and his men land on the island ruled by the witch Circe, who—weaving at an enormous loom—is *Maya* incarnate. She transforms half of Odysseus' men into pigs, symbolizing their total defeat at the hands of the lower passions, but also the dawning of *discernment*, the power to distinguish between the impulses of the lower self and those aspects of the psyche that may properly be called human. But Odysseus, the center of the spiritual Heart, is not overcome. Hermes provides him with a "sobriety drug", an "anti-illusionogenic" called *moly* (Ethiopian coffee, perhaps?) which is the exact opposite of the drug taken by the Lotus Eaters. Moly is the power of spiritual vigilance; it is this that allows him to overcome Circe's spells and turn his pigs back into men. And precisely *because* Odysseus resists her charms, Circe falls in love with him; when the contemplative "Center in the midst of conditions" is established and maintained, the manifest, conditional world turns to serve that Center. This is the great enantiodromia, where *avidya-maya* is changed into *vidya-maya*; Circe is here transformed from the *Maya* that deludes Odysseus into the *Shakti* that empowers and serves him. From now on she is not an enchantress, but a guide.

(7) Circe now sends Odysseus to the western edge of the world, the limit of manifestation beyond which nothing remains but the One, where he invokes the shade of the seer Tiresias. Tiresias had been transformed into a woman by the goddess Hera for a period of years, for the crime of striking a pair of copulating snakes with a staff. Later she strikes him blind as well, but gives him in return the gift of foresight. The striking of the snakes with the staff invokes the caduceus of Hermes, who also has an hermaphroditic aspect. The caduceus represents the power to unite opposites, as the *ida* and the *pingala*, the masculine and feminine psychic currents (the two

snakes), are united by being woven around the central *sushumna*, the *axis mundi*, in the practice of *kundalini-yoga*. Tiresias, having been changed from a man into a woman and back again, is beyond the pairs-of-opposites which are the warp and the weft of the world illusion. He is blind (like Homer was) to the multiplicity of this world, but his gift of foresight shows him the final end of the spiritual Path. He advises Odysseus on how to travel that Path to reach the ultimate goal.

After Tiresias, Odysseus speaks with the shade of his mother, who reveals to him the plight of his wife Penelope, beset by unwanted suitors in Ithaca, and he also encounters the shade of Agamemnon, who tells him of his own murder at the hands of his wife Clytemnestra. Here the necessity of completing the spiritual Path is revealed, along with the final destiny of all who fail to complete it: division and death, in a world woven on nothing but division and death—the world of the double cloak.

Odysseus and his men return to Circe's island where she advises them further on the journey ahead, and they set sail again.

(8) Odysseus and his men encounter the Sirens, symbols of the delusive and destructive side of spiritual Beauty—*al-Jamal, al-Malakut*—whose beautiful songs lure sailors to death on the rocks. His men put wax in their ears so they will not hear the Sirens' songs, but Odysseus asks to be tied to his ship's mast—the *axis mundi* again—so as to be able to hear the songs, while being restrained from following them. The lesson here is that only those who have fully attained the centrality of the human form can witness the Beauty of God and the esoteric secrets of the spiritual Path without being led to destruction. The Beauty and Mystery of the Divine are gifts that come in their own time; to run after them and try to grasp them—like the lustful brave, in Lakota myth, who wanted to rape the beautiful emissary of Wakan Tanka, White Buffalo Cow Woman—is to be destroyed by *al-Jalal*, the Majesty of God.

(9) Next the voyagers encounter Scylla, a many-headed sea-monster, and Charybdis, a whirlpool. The whirlpool is *samsara* (often compared to a whirlpool by the Buddhists), the engulfing and obliterating power of the world of relativity and formal manifestation; the sea-monster is the division of the soul—mind, affections and

will—between many worldly concerns, each of which takes a piece of us. Odysseus chooses to brave Scylla instead of falling into Charybdis, losing only six men (perhaps corresponding to the Six Lokas of samsaric existence in the Buddhist Kalachakra, or the six directions of space withdrawn into the Center) instead of the entire ship, and thereby demonstrating that even though the struggle with worldly necessity wounds us, to ignore it is fatal, and that passing beyond the pairs-of-opposites is not accomplished by failing to distinguish between them, but by choosing always "the lesser of two evils". One does not transcend good and evil by treating them as if they were the same thing, but by always choosing the good, at whatever cost, until the Sovereign Good is won—that Good which lies beyond the opposition of good and evil because, being all good, it has no opposite.

(10) The voyagers now land on the Island of Trinacis, where—contrary to the advice of both Circe and Tiresias—Odysseus' men hunt and slaughter the Cattle of the Sun. In punishment, all are drowned in a shipwreck except Odysseus, who is washed up half dead on the island of the goddess Calypso, where he must remain as her lover for seven years. The Cattle of the Sun represent a glimpse into the Divine Intellect and the Majesty of God—*al-Jalal, al-Jabarut*—producing a spiritual exaltation that the ego attempts to appropriate, ultimately resulting in a titanic inflation and fall. Odysseus is back in the clutches of this world—the nymph Calypso. Nonetheless, though he seems to have been defeated, the merit he gained through his earlier spiritual victories is still working in secret.

(11) Hermes now appears, and convinces Calypso to let Odysseus go; where spiritual *works* (necessary but not sufficient) must fail, the power of *grace* intervenes. So he builds a raft and sails to the island of Scherie. He is washed up on the beach exhausted, and there encounters the princess Nausicaa, symbol of *vidya-maya*. She introduces him to her parents, the rulers of the island (who are a foreshadowing of his reunion with Penelope), and when he tells them the story of his journey they decide to help him. With their aid he returns to Ithaca, disguised as a *swineherd*—as one who has gained the power to control the impulses of his lower self.

(12) Odysseus, in Ithaca, is recognized by his old housekeeper due to a scar on his thigh he received in his youth from a wild boar.

Homer, Poet of Maya

[NOTE: A friend of mine (a poet) once showed me, as a more-or-less magical object, a stone taken from the barrow-tomb known as The Grave of Queen Maeve, in Ireland. That night I dreamt I was a sacred swineherd; a boar came and slashed the outside of my right thigh, two or three inches above the knee—a wound I later identified as the wound of Odysseus. This dream took place on the night of the first full moon after the winter solstice—the one night of the year, according to Robert Graves in *The White Goddess*, when the ancient Egyptians ritually consumed swine-flesh.]

Odysseus enters his palace, still in disguise. The next day Athene prompts Penelope to issue a challenge to the suitors: to string Odysseus' bow and shoot through the holes of twelve axes placed in a row (These holes are sometimes called "helve-holes," as if they were holes in the hafts of the axes by which they could be hung on a wall, but I see them rather as the semi-circular spaces between the two upward-curving corners of the Cretan double-axe.) None of the suitors can even string the bow, but Odysseus can; he shoots an arrow through the holes of the twelve axes and wins the contest. He kills all the suitors, as well as the twelve maids who slept with them. He reveals himself to Penelope, who is uncertain of his identity until he describes the bed he built for her when they were first married. They are reunited.

The axes through which Odysseus shoots are double-headed axes with crescent blades, representing the waxing and waning phases of the Moon, the waning phases symbolizing the fall into the darkness of this world, under the power of *avidya-maya*, and the waxing phases the stations of the spiritual Path, by the power of *vidya-maya*. According to the *Bhagavad-Gita*, darkened souls destined for rebirth enter the waning Moon after death, while sanctified souls destined for Liberation enter the waxing Moon, and from there pass on through the Door of the Sun. And in Sufi symbolism, the double axe represents the cutting off of attachment both to this world and the next, leading to the realization of God not after death, but in this very life.

The twelve axes, which are twelve moons or months, are a *zodiac*, an entire cycle of manifestation, like the twelve gates of the Heavenly Jerusalem and the twelve stations of the Odyssey itself. That the twelve maids who slept with the suitors are killed symbolizes a passing beyond the sphere of the Moon, the cycles of nature and rebirth, and a realization of full Enlightenment. The number of Penelope's suitors is 108, a sacred number in Hindu and Buddhist lore. The suitors symbolize the level where worldly multiplicity is always seeking the blessing of spiritual Unity, perpetually struggling to possess the One without first *becoming* the One—an impossible task. When this level is killed, only Unity remains. The pre-eternal Unity, symbolized by the marriage-bed of Odysseus and Penelope, that held sway before Principle and Manifestation were polarized, is re-established; the spiritual Path is complete.

This is the secret Orpheus knew.

[NOTE: Buddhist mathematician Koenraad Elst explains that the number 108, considered purely in mathematical (not necessarily mythological) terms, is the principle of ontological hierarchy, of total possibility, and of repeating pattern. It might be called the number of *kosmos*; in the *Odyssey* it would seem to represent *kosmos* considered as *samsara*, as the round of births and deaths (the round of the circling spheres, the generation of repeating patterns in astronomical and human and biological life—i.e., *reincarnation*) that the philosophical character or spiritual hero seeks to be liberated from. He says:

> [Given the division of the circle into 360 degrees], the angle of 108 has a unique property: the ratio between the straight line uniting two points at 108 degrees from each other on a circle's circumference (in effect, one of the sides of a 10-pointed star) and the radius of that circle equals the Golden Section. Likewise, the inside of every angle of a pentagon measures 108 degrees, and the pentagon is a veritable embodiment of the Golden Section, e.g., the ratio between a side of the 5-pointed star and a side of the pentagon is the Golden Section. . . . The Golden Section means a proportion between two magnitudes, the major and the minor, such that the minor is to the major as the major is to the whole, i.e., to the sum of minor and major. In living nature, there are plenty of sequences where every member stands to the preceding member in a Golden Proportion or its derivatives (square root etc.), e.g., the distances between or the sizes of the successive twigs growing on a branch,

the layers of petals on a flower, the rings of a conch, the generations of a multiplying rabbit population, etc. What this symbolizes is the law of invariance: in every stage of a development, the same pattern repeats itself. The son is to the father as the father was to the grandfather. Wheels within wheels: every whole consisting of parts is itself likewise part of a larger whole. And the principle of order: the underling obeys the orders of his master to the same extent that the master obeys the requirements of the whole ... 9 is the Hindu number of planets, and 12 is the Zodiac, so 108 is the total number of planet-in-Zodiacal-sign combinations. This makes it into the total set of all possible planetary influences taken separately, or in a more generalized symbolism, the matrix containing all possibilities.]

[http://koenraadelst.bharatvani.org/articles/misc/why108.html]

7

The Metaphysical Uses of Metaphor, Kenning, Riddle and Rune in the Teutonic Tradition

for Henrik Palmgren

ACCORDING to the genealogy of the Baskerville family (a tributary to my mother's family, the Strothers), compiled by P. Hamilton Baskerville of Richmond, Virginia, and supplemented by the Strother family genealogy put together by my great aunt (both families are Norman), I am descended from the Anglo-Saxon god Woden, the god of "Wednesday", whom the Norse knew as Odin. But how, in today's world, does one manage to be descended from a god? Did one of the daughters of men, some ancestress of mine, mate with one of the Sons of God who looked upon her and found her fair? The reality was less spectacular. As we learn from the *Prose* or *Younger Edda* of Snorri Sturluson, when the Norse tribes were Christianized, those skalds (poets) who, like Snorri, wanted to preserve the heroic tales of the Aesir upon which the poetic traditions of the Northmen were based, demoted them from gods to ancestors. According to the story recounted in the *Younger Edda*, Odin—like Aeneas, the progenitor of the Latins, and Brutus, the ancestor of the Kings of Britain, according to Virgil and Geoffrey of Monmouth respectively—was a Trojan. He migrated from Troy to the Norse lands in response to a vision informing him that he would meet a greater destiny in Scandinavia than in Asia Minor; he followed its guidance and became the ancestor of the Scandinavian kings. In line with this "contra-euhemerization", the Baskerville genealogy gives the ancestry of King Alfred the Great as coming down from

Adam, through the line of the patriarchs chronicled in the Book of Genesis, as far as Noah, after which the Hebrew patriarchal names suddenly become Anglo-Saxon ones, beginning with Sceaf or Streaf—who, as a note informs us, was "born in the Ark" (and how appropriate this is for a figure who might be characterized as the "proto-Viking"!). Sixteenth in line from Sceaf is Woden, and "from him proceeded the kings of many nations"; twenty-third in line from Woden is Alfred. This hybrid genealogy, based on the *Saxon Chronicles* first collected under Alfred the Great in the 9th century, was undoubtedly composed by Saxon/Christian monks in an attempt to square the ancestor-lore of the Teutons with the Judeo-Christian Bible.

When Woden or Odin, the chief god of the Teutons, was first encountered by the Romans, they syncretized him with the Roman god Mercury, master of eloquence and guide of souls to the upper and lower worlds, who was sometimes pictured as androgenous in nature. They undoubtedly did this in part because Odin was the first and only one of the Aesir to obtain the Runes, the letters and/or archetypal cosmological symbols of the Norse alphabet. Likewise— as Robert Graves informs us in *The White Goddess*—Mercury, according to a fable of Hyginus, invented the first seven letters of the alphabet after watching a flight of cranes, "which make letters as they fly". Furthermore, Odin had to sacrifice his right eye to gain possession of the Runes, thus making him a *divided* being, a case of the *coincidentia oppositorum* or union of opposites, like the hermaphroditic Mercury. A divided being is crucified on the tree of duality, like Odin on Yggdrasill or Christ on the Cross. It is by virtue of the suffering of this very self-division, which manifests also as a division between self and world, that dualism is transcended and the Transcendent Unity of Being attained; as W. B. Yeats says in his poem "Crazy Jane Talks with the Bishop": "For nothing can be sole or whole / That has not been rent." It was through this kind and degree of suffering that the two natures of Christ, the human and the Divine, perfected their Hypostatic Union in the world of time, thus opening a doorway to that Union as it already existed, in the world of Eternity. When a being from a higher world incarnates in this lower one, cruel division, and the final healing of that division in a greater Unity, become that being's destiny. Ymir, the original Giant in Norse mythology, and Purusha, the original Person in the Hindu universe, were slaughtered to create the world: their blood became the rivers, their bones the mountains, etc. The same was true of Christ, whom St. John characterizes as the One without whom "nothing was made that has been made" (John 1:1), who is called "the Lamb slain from the foundation of the world" (Revelations 3:6), and who, when instituting the Eucharist, "took bread, and gave thanks, and broke it, and gave to them, saying, This is my body which is given for you: this do in remembrance of Me" (Luke 22:19). But it is in Christ that we can more clearly see the ultimate re-unification of what has been divided: "That they all may be one; as thou, Father, in me, and I in thee, that they also may be one in us" (John 17:21). The "remembrance of Me" He spoke of at the Last Supper was not simply a reminiscence, but a *re-membering* of His Body which was about to be dis-membered at His coming Crucifixion—just as it already had been from the foundation of the world, precisely so as to found it. (Perhaps we should remember at this point that the Norse accepted Christianity from the missionaries without invasion or external coercion—though certainly not without popular resistance, as witness the forceful imposition of the faith by King Olaf Tryggvason of Norway. Nonetheless they undoubtedly recognized a number of parallels between Jesus Christ and the Odin they knew; and the fact is that certain rune-stones are inscribed with a figure who might be either Odin or Jesus. The Christian church came to those who were open to it as a fuller and fresher revelation of the ancient Way of things—the Way St. Augustine was referring to when he said that Christianity has always existed, but has only been known by that name since the coming of Jesus Christ.)

Odin obtained the Runes by hanging for nine days and nights, as a sacrifice to himself, on the world tree of Yggdrasill, the *axis mundi*. In the words of the *Poetic* or *Elder Edda*,

> I ween that I hung on the windy tree,
> Hung there for nights full nine;
> With the spear I was wounded, and offered I was

To Othin, myself to myself,
On the tree that none may ever know
What root beneath it runs.

Yggdrasill was planted above a well known as the Well of Urd or Udr, who was one of the three *Norns* or Fates of the Norse—Udr, Verdandi and Skuld—the one who represented knowledge of the past—of the Origins. In other versions of the myth this well is known as Mimir's Well; Mimir was a mysterious omniscient being whose name means "Memory". Likewise the Nine Greek Muses, who are in some ways akin to the three Moirae or Fates—almost as if they were the "Moirae squared"—are called the Daughters of Memory, or *Mnemosyne*. Memory in this sense is more than simple reminiscence; it is akin to the *anamnesis* of the Platonists, the remembrance of the Divine Reality, which is the basis of the Sufi method of *dhikru Allah* and the Eastern Orthodox Christian practice of *mnimi Theou*, both of which mean "remembrance of God". Odin was wounded with his own spear during his ordeal and, according to one version of the story, suffered from thirst. Likewise Christ on the Cross said "I thirst" and was pierced by the spear of Longinus. And just as Odin was sacrificed to himself, so Christ, according to St. Anselm's doctrine that the Son willingly offered himself to the Father so as to satisfy the Divine Wrath that had fallen on humanity due to Adam's sin, was also sacrificed to "himself", seeing that the Nicene Creed describes the Son as "of one substance with the Father". According to another version of the myth, Odin gouged out one of his eyes as an offering to Mimir, reminding us of Christ's words in Matthew 18:9, "if thine eye offend thee, pluck it out, and cast it from thee"; after he dropped it into Mimir's Well, its occupant gave him water to drink—water which was Wisdom. It was through this sacrifice that Odin obtained the Runes, the understanding of the eternal metaphysical principles underlying cosmic manifestation. And although Odin was a god, one of the Aesir, this legend presents him as undergoing, precisely, a kind of shamanic initiatory ordeal; and it is true that Odin was considered to be the Great Magician as well as the chief of the gods. Here we can see that Snorri Sturluson's transformation of the Aesir from gods into human ancestors may have been more than a convert's concession to Christian doctrine so as to retain his cultural heritage in diminished form; his "contra-euhemerization" may in fact have been based on an earlier euhemerization by which the warriors and sages of the Norse limb of the great Indo-European past were raised, via apotheosis, to the status of gods, like the heroes of the Greeks or the Hindu *rishis*.

In the Islamic version of this mythologem, the one-eyed power appears in the figure of *al-Dajjal*, "the Deceiver", the Antichrist. Given that the left eye sees this world and the right eye the next (or vice-versa), *al-Dajjal* is blind to the next world and sees only this one; he is thus the *archetypal materialist*. In Odin, however, the one-eyed motif has the opposite meaning. Instead of seeing this world with both eyes, the loss of his right eye gives him the power to see the other world as well, as if the now-invisible eye were turned backward in his head to behold the invisible world. In poetic terms, this ability to see one thing as two and two things as one—to distinguish between the visible and invisible worlds so as to synthesize them on a higher level—is, precisely, the origin of *metaphor*. (When Jesus Christ said "If your eye become single, your whole body will be filled with light" (Matthew 6:22), he was giving us another version of the one-eyed motif as symbolic of higher consciousness, like the *ajña-chakra* or "third eye" of the Hindu yogis. *Cerebral* consciousness is dualistic, but *cardiac* consciousness is unitary. The two eyes in the head see this world and the next as divided; the Eye of the Heart sees them as one.)

So the poetic and contemplative use of metaphor is precisely to present a given object as simultaneously occupying this world and the next; in so doing it allows the poet to render (in Frithjof Schuon's phrase) "the metaphysical transparency of phenomena." In the world of metaphor, one thing is two things, and those two things, one. In the traditional Catholic Litany of the Blessed Virgin, Mary is called Seat of Wisdom, Tower of Ivory, House of Gold, Morning Star. This is pure *metaphor*, the Greek word for "carrying over" or "carrying beyond". In our mind's eye we see a Tower of Ivory that is simultaneously a beautiful woman, a beautiful woman who is simultaneously a House of Gold or the Morning Star. This doubling of the object renders it *apparitional*, thereby destroying the literalism that would "take it for granted", degrading it to the level of a possession and aspect of the ego. The letter, or literalism, killeth; the Spirit, or *metaphor*, giveth life (cf. 2 Corinthians 3:6). In the traditional—that is, the magical and symbolist—understanding of human language, to name something is to invoke it, to make it present, to actually summon it. Yet the primordial poet/magicians who first heard the actual Word of God were also very careful not to confuse the object with the verbal designation for it; as Shakespeare put it, repeating the ancient warning not to be fooled by the magic of human language, "A rose by any other name would smell as sweet." As in the world of metaphor, an object is simultaneously one with its name and also distinct from it. If it were not identifiable with its name we would not be able to *call* it; if it were not also distinguishable from its name it would be sunk in literalism, in taken-for-grantedness—too heavy, dull and opaque to hear and respond to its own name when we call it out from the inarticulate darkness around it. Only when literal things are transformed into apparitions, and apparitions into *real* things, can the art of poetry, and the art of magic, do their work.

In terms of the poetic tradition of the Norse and the Anglo-Saxons, the hoard of stock metaphors kept in store by the skalds were known as *kennings,* a word undoubtedly related to the Scottish and Old English verb "to ken" meaning "to know"; *kennings* are *knowings.* They are a common device in the Icelandic *sagas* and the Anglo-Saxon epic *Beowulf.* Among the kennings for *sword* according to Sturluson are "worm-borer" and "werwolf" and "corpse-maker" and "gate-flame"; those for *sea* include "emptiness", "sucker", "swallower", "brawler" and "whale's-acre". It is as if, in order to really *know* or *ken* something, you need to see it as other than itself and call it by a different name. This is undoubtedly due to the fact that polarity is the principle of all manifestation. A thing can only appear when contrasted with something other than it, something unlike it, without which the figure-ground polarity cannot come into play. For a thing to *exist* means (in Latin) for it to "stand out" from its surroundings; consequently, as Plotinus taught, the act of creation is inseparable from the act of perception, a truth we express when we say things like "I finally *made her out* on the hillside yonder." When

we strictly identify a thing with our common name for it we suc-
cumb to the temptation of thinking we already know everything
about it, and consequently that we need pay no attention to it whatsoever. But if a *sword* is also a *werwolf*, then we have been alerted to
the fact that every object, experience, situation and moment contains infinitely more than we ever suspected, things that we ignore
only at our peril—each of which is worthy of the familiar piece of
folk wit, "if it'd been a snake it would've bit me." (Many of the things
we now call *clichés* are masterpieces of wit that when first hatched
were recognized as brilliant—as witness "more than you could shake
a stick at" or "loading mercury with a pitchfork".) Metaphor, then, is
not just accidental decoration, much less the deliberate obscurity
the Philistine suspects when he complains, "why doesn't that poet
just say what he means?" It is hyper-vigilance, a kind of x-ray vision.
It is a tool designed to deepen and enhance metaphysical contemplation.

Related to the metaphor is the *riddle*, which is found in both
Anglo-Saxon poetry and some traditional English ballads—"Green
Grow the Rushes-o", for example, or "Scarborough Faire". For some
reason we now class riddles as jokes, and see any riddle that doesn't
make us laugh as an unsuccessful example of the genre. But to the
Anglo-Saxon or Norse poet learning his craft, the riddle was a sober
and serious exercise in seeing one thing as another, first in order to
penetrate beyond the surface of things into their central mystery,
secondly to learn how to construct new metaphors so as to deepen
and embellish his art. Here are four examples of Anglo-Saxon riddles, which were undoubtedly posed to apprentice poets as a train-
ing device; I've taken them from the Penguin edition of *The Earliest
English Poems*, translated by Michael Alexander, 1966:

> The thing is magic, unimaginable
> To him who knows not how it is.
> It throstles through its sides, its throat angled,
> And turned with knowledge, two barrels
> Set sharp on the shoulder.
>   Its shaping is fulfilled
> As it stands by the wayside so wonderful to see,
> Tall and gleaming, to glad the passer-by.

I was in one hour an ashen crone,
A fair-faced man, a fresh girl,
Floated on foam, flew with birds,
Under the wave dived, dead among fish
And walked upon land a living soul.

I heard of a wonder, of words moth-eaten;
That is a strange thing, I thought, weird
That a man's song be swallowed by a worm,
His binded sentences, his bedside stand-by,
Rustled in the night—and the robber guest
Not one whit the wiser for the words he had mumbled.

❖

I saw a woman
Sit alone.

I'll let the first three remain mysteries for the reader, as some still are to me, in view of William Blake's observation that "The wisest of the Ancients consider'd what is not too Explicit as the fittest for Instruction because it rouzes the faculties to act"—but number four can have only one true answer: the Full Moon. To solve this riddle the poet or exegete must allow a simple image to carry *itself* over into metaphor, doubling and re-unifying itself of its own accord. Thus poetry not only trains the imagination, but places that imagination at the service of metaphysical vision, thereby revealing the poet's courting of the Muse to be one more in the catalogue of traditional contemplative techniques.

In addition to riddle and metaphor, poetic language can be used to understand, approach, express and invoke metaphysical truth by virtue of the essential sounds of human speech, both in terms of their physiological resonances and of the archetypal meanings attributed to them. In the Teutonic tradition this science was based on a working knowledge of the Runes.

The Elder Futhark or Runic alphabet of 24 characters is divided into three Aetts (eights), the first of which is under the patronage of the god Freyr and/or his sister Freya. This Aett represents the metaphysical order expressed cosmologically in terms of what the Greeks called *proödos* and *epistrophe*, Creation and Return.

The first rune, Fehu (cattle, wealth), represents *materia* or Substance, the primal feminine power. The second rune, Uruz (the aurochs—the gigantic wild ox, now extinct) symbolizes *forma* or Essence, the primal masculine power. The union of these two releases the tremendous energy of Creation symbolized by the rune Thuriaz (thorn or giant), the rune of Thor. The fourth rune, Ansuz, (breath, the primal god)—the rune of Woden or Odin—is the symbol of the universal system of Creation that is established after the energy of Thuriaz is ordered and rendered intelligible by the power of the Runes; the transition from Thuriaz to Ansuz is analogous to the defeat of the Titans and the establishment of the Olympian order of the Gods in the Greek tradition. This completes the movement of Creation.

Raidho (chariot, travel), the fifth rune, is the beginning of the path of return to Source, based on the appearance and activation of the human psychophysical vehicle, which is symbolized by a chariot in several traditions. The sixth rune, Kenaz (torch) represents the kindling of Knowledge in the sense of spiritual illumination. Gebo (gift), the seventh rune, symbolizes the sacrifice of ego and the corresponding invocation of divine providence. Lastly, the eighth rune, Wunjo (joy) stands for the fulfillment that is achieved, and given, upon completion of the Spiritual Path. This finishes the movement of Return.

> Fehu's the stuff,
> Uruz, the shaft,
> Thuriaz the thunder
> When earth meets sky,
> Ansuz the dawn
> Where at peace we lie.
>
> Raidho's what we ride
> Through Kenaz, what we ken,
> To Gebo where we give up

All we've got—
Then Wunjo arrives,
Unloads our golden lot.

The meanings of the succeeding sixteen runes are equally archetypal. Imagine the poetic effects that were possible when every letter
of every word—and every sound in human speech—was recognized as embodying and invoking a specific archetypal energy,
something on the order of the "seed-syllables" in the Hindu science
of *mantra*. This should give us some idea of the power represented
by the full poetic command of human language in the first ages of
the world.

8

Metaphysical Lore
in Traditional Ballads

This essay is more-or-less a continuation of the material presented in *Folk Metaphysics: Mystical Meanings in Traditional Folk Songs and Spirituals*, Sophia Perennis, 2005

ANYONE familiar with the language of metaphysics, as well as with the particular dialect of that language known as *mythopoesis*, will easily understand (as soon as they turn their eyes in the right direction) that certain traditional folk songs are actually tight, consciously-composed little metaphysical essays. "Scarborough Fair", for example, is the story of God's quest for the human soul exiled in this lower world, while "The Lady Gay" treats of the lesser mysteries situated within the order of nature, versus the greater mysteries which transcend that order.

Ananda K. Coomaraswamy has this to say about folklore as metaphysics:

> By "folklore" we mean that whole and consistent body of culture which has been handed down, not in books but by word of mouth and in practice, from time beyond the reach of historical research, in the form of legends, fairy tales, ballads, games, toys, crafts, medicine, agriculture, and other rites, and forms of organization, especially those we call tribal. This is a cultural complex independent of national and even racial boundaries, and of remarkable similarity throughout the world. . . .
>
> The content of folklore is metaphysical. Our failure to recognize this is primarily due to our own abysmal ignorance of metaphysics and of its technical terms. . . .
>
> Folklore ideas are the form in which metaphysical doctrines are

66

received by the people and transmitted by them. In its popular form, a given doctrine may not always have been understood, but so long as the formula is faithfully transmitted it remains understandable; "superstitions", for the most part, are no mere delusions, but formulae of which the meaning has been forgotten. . . .

We are dealing with the relics of an ancient *wisdom*, as valid now as it ever was. . . . We shall only be able to understand the astounding uniformity of the folklore motifs all over the world, and the devoted care that has everywhere been taken to ensure their correct transmission, if we approach these *mysteries* (for they are nothing less) in the spirit in which they have been transmitted ("from the Stone Age until now")—with the confidence of little children, indeed, but not the childish self-confidence of those who hold that wisdom was born with themselves. The true folklorist must be not so much a psychologist as a theologian and metaphysician, if he is to "understand his material". . . . Nor can anything be called a *science* of folklore, but only a collection of data, that considers only the formulae and not their doctrine. . . . [*Coomaraswamy, Selected Papers, 1: Traditional Art and Symbolism*, edited by Roger Lipsey, Princeton University Press, 1977]

But if some traditional ballads are actually consciously-constructed metaphysical essays, then who composed them? René Guénon gives us part of the answer:

The very conception of *folklore*, in the generally accepted sense of the term, is based on an idea that is radically false, the idea that there are "popular creations" spontaneously created by the mass of the people. . . . As has been rightly said [by Luc Benoist], "the profound interest of all so-called popular traditions lies in the fact that they are not popular in origin"; and we will add that where, as is almost always the case, there is a question of elements that are traditional in the true sense of the word, however deformed, diminished and fragmentary they may be sometimes, and of things that have a real symbolic value, their origin is not even human, let alone popular. What may be popular is solely the fact of "survival," when these elements belong to vanished traditional forms. . . . The people preserve, without understanding them, the relics of former traditions which go back sometimes to a past too remote to be dated, so that it has to be relegated to the obscure domain of the "prehistoric"; they thereby fulfill the function of a

more or less subconscious collective memory, the contents of
which have clearly come from elsewhere. What may seem most
surprising is that the things so preserved are found to contain,
above all, abundant information of an esoteric order, which is, in
its essence, precisely what is least popular, and this fact suggests in
itself an explanation, which may be summed up as follows: When
a traditional form is on the point of becoming extinct, its last representatives may very well deliberately entrust to this aforesaid
collective memory the things that otherwise would be lost beyond
recall; that is in fact the sole means of saving what can in a certain
measure be saved. At the same time, that lack of understanding
that is one of the natural characteristics of the masses is a sure
enough guarantee that what is esoteric will be nonetheless undi-
vulged, remaining merely as a sort of witness of the past for such
as, in later times, shall be capable of understanding it. [*Symbols of
the Sacred Science*, Sophia Perennis, 2004]

Here, following these two masters, is my attempt to discern the
metaphysical symbolism in five traditional folk songs, one carol,
and one "literary ballad" composed in the style and spirit of the traditional ballad.

ONE

"Son David"—to Die Before you Die

The ballad "Son David", as sung by June Tabor and Oysterband on
their album *The Ragged Kingdom* [http://www.youtube.com/watch
?v=XILzqPc5P5g], ultimately derives from the Child ballads; it's a
song about the spiritual Path, about "death in life and life in death".
Here are the lyrics:

What's the blood on the point of your sword?
O Son David, my Son David,
What's the blood on the point of your sword?
Promise, tell me true.

That's the blood of my grey mare
O Lady Mother, my Lady Mother,
That's the blood of my grey mare
She would not rule by me.

Your grey mare's blood was never so red
   O Son David, my Son David,
Your grey mare's blood was never so red
   Its promise tell me true.

That's the blood of my hawking hound
   O Lady Mother, my Lady Mother,
That's the blood of my hawking hound
   She would not rule by me.

Your hawking hound's blood was never so clear
   O Son David, my Son David,
Your hawking hound's blood was never so clear
   Its promise tell me true.

That's the blood of my brother John
   O Lady Mother, my Lady Mother,
That's the blood of my brother John
   He drew his sword to me.

What did you fall out about
   O Son David, my Son David?
It's all for a little holly bush
   That'll never grow to a tree.

I'll set my foot on a bottomless boat
   O Lady Mother, my Lady Mother,
Set my foot on a bottomless boat,
   Sail upon the sea.

When will you come back again?
   O Son David, my Son David
When will you come back again?
   Its promise tell me true.

When the Sun and Moon meet in yonder glen
   O Lady Mother, my Lady Mother,
Sun and Moon meet in yonder glen,
   And that will never be.

It sounds as if Son David never really killed his grey mare and his hawking hound, but since the song pictures these actions, in a way they really take place. To kill your mare is to mortify your body, your instincts; to kill your hawking hound is to mortify your mind.

A "hawking hound" would be a retriever. The falconer hunts with hawk and hound; the hawk brings down the bird, the hound retrieves it. So to kill the hawking hound would be to kill something like intellectual greed or acquisitiveness; birds are thoughts. And to kill your brother is to mortify *yourself* (your ego, your mirror-image); these are the three main stages of the spiritual Path. When the Lady Mother says, "your grey mare's blood was never so red; your hawking hound's blood was never so clear", she's alluding to the redness of the passions and the clarity of the intellect. Both mare and hound must be ruled; both must ultimately be killed. This is as much as "I" can do, with the help of God, but it's not the final thing—because ultimately "I" too must die.

Robert Graves in *The White Goddess* recounts songs and poems where Holly is said to be the best of trees: "Of all the trees whatsoever the critically best is holly" says "Song of the Forest Trees"; and "The Holly-Tree Carol" sings: "Of all the trees that are in the wood, the Holly bears the crown"—the crown of thorns. "Holly" means "Holy". It is sometimes conflated with the evergreen Oak, the bloody Oak whose bark is used for tanning (which means, for preserving, for making immortal; "the tanner is his twin's executioner", says Graves)—the crucifixion tree that rules the waning half of the year after the summer solstice. Holly stands for the letter T in the Beth-Luis-Nion Tree Alphabet, which in Latin script takes the shape of the Tau-cross where the serpent of the passions is nailed—the percussive consonant that makes the sound of a hammer. So it's the tree of the spiritual Path, of the self-annihilation the Sufis call *fana'*, the return from manifest existence to invisible Source. If it never grows to a tree, this means in one sense that the spiritual impulse is cut short by bloodshed, at least in this world; if holiness can be claimed only by murder, then what self, what ego, can claim it? But in another sense it refers to something that, being evergreen, is not only deathless but ever-young. The conflict between brothers represents the world of the *dvandvas*, the pairs-of-opposites, the Tree of the Knowledge of Good and Evil. But behind the Tree of Knowledge, beyond all dualities, lies the evergreen Holly, the Tree of Life; it will never *grow* to a tree because it is beyond all growth and decay. So Son David, having transcended all opposition, can now cross the Ocean of Existence to the farther shore, the other world. Externally the song is a tragedy; esoterically it's a song of spiritual hope; it calls up all our latent despair, but it also hides a precious jewel. "The Secret protects itself", yes, but all that obscures the Secret also has to be called up, so it can be dispelled. Brother-murder, the desperate and violent attempt to transcend oneself, is negative in many ways; in Sufi terms it's the *nafs al-lawwama*, the "accusing self", the troubled conscience, which is certainly the state of Son David in the song. It's also the condition alluded to by Jesus in Matthew 11:12: "And from the days of John the Baptist until now, the kingdom of heaven suffereth violence, and the violent bear it away". Yet it initiates the impulse that carries the spiritual traveler across the sea by the power of the wind, the Spirit. When I asked my wife Jenny what "bottomless boat" might mean, she said: "To sail in a bottomless boat is to sail with the power of the Infinite itself"—so the boat is the spiritual Path. And the glen is *al-Qalb*, the Sufi term for the spiritual Heart, where *ar-Ruh*, the Spirit (symbolized by the Sun) and *an-nafs al-mutma'inna*, the self-at-peace, the soul receptive and submissive to God, (symbolized by the Moon), marry; in the Qur'an (like in that Dürer print of the Apocalypse), the union of Sun and Moon is a sign of the Day of Resurrection. The marriage of Sun and Moon represents the reconciliation of the two brothers, David and John, *ar-Ruh* and *an-Nafs*, Spirit and Soul, in a higher dimension—just as, in Judaism, Jacob the spiritual man and Esau the natural man are reconciled on the Feast of Tabernacles, which takes place in a rural setting, or an imitation of one, in "yonder glen"—the very glen where Yeats hoped to "walk among long dappled grass", and finally taste "the silver apples of the Moon, the golden apples of the Sun."

But who is the Lady Mother? She is somehow the Witness of the whole action, and also the one who strips you of lies and illusions, and in whose presence you must tell the truth. And at each revelation of new depths of destruction, and potential salvation, by Son David, her questioning challenge remains the same: *Its promise tell me true*—as if each event in life, arising out of relentless fatality, were no more than a riddle to be solved, an enigma veiling a spiritual potential: and that's the simple truth. So She is related to the

Hebrew Shekhina, the Divine Immanence, the mysterious Will and Presence of God in this world, which is also in some ways the function of the Virgin Mary in her role as Mediatrix. She's the one who sees the blood on the tip of the sword and knows what it is; she's the one to whom Son David will return when "Sun and Moon meet in yonder glen", which is also *al-Jannah*, the Garden of Paradise, symbol of Divine Knowledge. The action of the ballad, the crime that's really the greatest good fortune, the *felix culpa* or "fortunate fault", is both what carries the Son away from her and what returns him to her at last. As Jesus said, "He who seeks to maintain his life will lose it, but he who loses his life, for My sake, shall find it."

So the Lady Mother must be Sophia, Holy Wisdom. In Her uncompromising presence, only the Truth can be told. The lies we live in, and name with our names—she peels them off like skins with the lightning of Her gaze, with the blade of Her witness. This is essentially the same gift that the Queen of Elfland gives True Thomas in the ballad "Thomas Rymer":

> Syne they came on to a garden green,
>   And she pu'd an apple frae a tree:
> "Take this for thy wages, True Thomas [she said],
>   It will give the tongue that can never lee [lie]."

And when will Son David return to Her? Never in this world— but *never* is only the midnight side of *ever*. To say "that will never be" simply means that it will not, and has not, and cannot be in *this* world, the world of *time*. This is the secret affinity and identity between the Necessary and the Impossible. Union with God is obviously impossible to us; it is therefore inevitable, given that "with God all things are possible." It *will not be* because *it is*—forever, in God's Eternal Now. That "forever" is always here, like the ground under our feet; we walk upon it every day. In that sense, we never left the Garden.

Two Songs

The next two ballads appear on the album *Am I Born to Die?* by Mason Brown and Chipper Thompson. Some believe that "Going to the West" was composed in Appalachian America in the 19th century; Lyle Lofgren says: "This song was composed about 1880, when there was a large migration of people from the county (Marshall, in the hill country of northeastern Alabama) going to the new lands of Texas." If this is so, it goes to demonstrate how topical material can be grafted onto the root of earlier compositions that rise from a basically mythical substratum, and how this archetypal layer of meaning can lend a deeper resonance to songs that are consciously conceived of in strictly personal or contemporary terms.

TWO

"Going to the West"—
The Pilgrimage of the Soul

In this fair land I'll stay no more,
Your labor is in vain.
I'll leave the mountains of my birth
And seek the fertile plane.
I'm going
To the West.

You say you will not go with me,
You turn your eyes away.
You say you will not follow me
No matter what I say.
I'm going
To the West.

Three years have gone since we first met,
Since you became my bride.
Now I must journey far away
Without you by my side.
I'm going
To the West.

You say you will not go with me,
You turn your eyes away.
You say you will not follow me
No matter what I say.

I'm going
To the West.

I'll leave you here in this land you love
'Mid scenes so bright and fair,
Where fragrant flowers are blooming
And music fills the air.
I'm going
To the West.

You say you will not go with me,
You turn your eyes away.
You say you will not follow me
No matter what I say.
I'm going
To the West.

This ballad tells the story of the pilgrimage of the soul from "the mountains of my birth", the celestial world, west to "the fertile plane", this earthly world—"west" being the symbolic quarter of matter, the place where the Sun of the Spirit sets. That the bride of the pilgrim refuses to go west with him identifies her (in Zoroastrian terms) as his *fravashi* or *fravarti*—his celestial counterpart who never incarnates, never descends into material manifestation; by this she may be known as the sign and seal of his power to return to that higher world when his pilgrimage is done.

The number symbolism of the ballad confirms this interpretation. To say "Three years are gone / Since we first met / Since you became my bride / Now I must journey far away / Without you by my side" indicates a shift, at the beginning of the fourth year, from the celestial plane, universally symbolized by the number 3 (the Trinity in Christianity, the *Trimurti* in Hinduism, etc.) to the terrestrial plane, symbolized by the number 4 (the 4 seasons, the 4 directions, etc.).

This is a fall, but also a *felix culpa*, a "fortunate fault"—an exile, but also the inheritance of a kingdom. The incarnational descent from Heaven to Earth is a loss, but a loss in view of a greater gain. The earthly plane is not purely fallen; it is also "fertile", capable of receiving the seed of the Spirit; the pilgrim himself, in one sense, is this very seed: "Except a corn of wheat fall into the ground and die, it abideth alone: but if it die, it bringeth forth much fruit" (John 12:24). Ultimately, this fruit is the reunion of Heaven and Earth when the cycle of manifestation is complete.

THREE

"The Verdant Braes of Skreen"— *Maya* and Its Transcendence

This is a traditional Irish ballad in which the Hawthorn tree, well known as a sacred tree also in Wales, and in ancient Britain as a whole, figures prominently:

> As I went out one morning
> By the verdant braes of Skreen;
> I leaned against a hawthorn tree
> To view the Sun in the forest green.

> I spied a neat young fellow
> With a girl all on his knee,
> And he so smart and handsome was
> And she so fair and fine to see.

(*The young man speaks:*)

> "Come sit you down all on the ground
> On the dewy grass so green,
> For it's just been nine months my love
> Since you and I've together been."

(*The girl replies:*)

> "I'll not sit down all on the grass
> Nor be a love of thine,
> For I find you love a Kingston maid;
> Your heart no longer will be mine.

> "I'll not trust what an old man says,
> His days are well-nigh done;
> And I'll not trust a young man's word,
> He sets his eye on many's the one.

"But I will climb a tall, tall tree
And rob a wild bird's nest,
And I'll bring home what I do find
All to the arms that I love best."

As I went out one morning
By the verdant braes of Skreen;
I leaned against a hawthorn tree
To view the Sun in the forest green.

The first and last verses of this song tell of a man who goes out "one morning" to "view the Sun in the forest green." The "morning" places the action of the song nearer the archetypal realm than the "evening" would have, which (like the "west" in the first song) would symbolize the world of material manifestation. And "To view the Sun in the forest green" means, precisely, "To contemplate the Divine Intellect via its refraction in the Imaginal Plane"—the place where invisible, intelligible realities appear as symbolic images, as they did to the knight questing through the primeval forest in so many medieval romances.

In this song we are presented with a classic "May" scene of two young lovers in a leafy glade. And according to Robert Graves in *The White Goddess*, the hawthorn is the tree of the month of May, sacred to the goddess Maia—who is *Maya*. The hawthorn, paradoxically, is both orgiastic and symbolic of chastity. It is also inimical to marriage, as the orgiastic impulse most certainly is; until this impulse is tempered by chastity, no fertile marriage is possible. The young man wants to lay with his lover, but do so nine months after they first came together—precisely when, that is, she is about to give birth. And so she repudiates him—"exoterically" because she knows he has been unfaithful, but "esoterically" because she is about to go into labor. So who, or what, is she about to give birth to? The answer is, "Wisdom—the power to see through the veils of *Maya*, the world-illusion." And what does this Wisdom teach her? It teaches her to trust neither "what an old man's says", which has no force, nor "a young man's word", which has no center (though the phrase "many's the one" reminds us that the "many" actually *is* the "One", as obscured by our dissipation, our scattered and divided

76

attention). And when she declares that she trusts neither youth nor old age, it means that she no longer trusts *time*—time, which in the "natural" course of things is no more than a passage from force without wisdom to wisdom without force. Instead, she vows to rob the nest of a "tall, tall tree"—the Tree of Life, where Spirit lays its egg in a nest on the highest branch—and bring it "home" to the "arms that she loves best."

What precisely is "home" to the one who, having seen through the illusions of time, has given birth, after nine months, to her own higher self—who after the cycle of spiritual gestation is complete has reaped in Wisdom what was sown in passion? As William Blake wrote, in "The Mental Traveler":

> I traveled through a Land of Men
> A land of Men & Women too
> And heard & saw such dreadful things
> As cold earth wanderers never knew

> For there the Babe is born in joy
> That was begotten in dire woe
> Just as we Reap in joy the fruit
> Which we in bitter tears did sow

That home is Eternity. And whose are the arms that the girl who has brought forth Wisdom now loves best? They are God's. The Spirit is her true husband, not the "neat young fellow" in the forest (who is only one of His many masks, faithless as all masks are until recognized as such)—which is why she brings back to Him, not to the fickle young man, the *hiranyagharba*, the golden "Orphic" egg of total, primal manifestation.

The Glastonbury Thorn, a hawthorn tree, was sacred to the Virgin Mary, as is the holy ground of Glastonbury Abbey a whole. The Thorn had the peculiarity of flowering twice a year instead of once—on old wood in the Spring (as is normal), but also on new growth in the Winter season. *The Verdant Braes of Skreen* maps out the passage from Spring—from May, the Virgin's month and month of the hawthorn, symbolizing natural eros—to Winter, the season of transcendence, of the Northern or Hyperborean Mary, whose epithet "Star of the Sea" denotes the Pole Star, "the still point of the turning world", the gateway that leads from the cycles of cosmic manifestation to the eternity of the Spirit. And if the "tall, tall tree" whose nest the girl robs is in fact the hawthorn, then she has stolen the power of eros from the orgiastic aspect of that tree (the flower of Spring) and returned it to the chaste, spiritual, transcendent aspect (the flower of Winter). The hawthorn in flower is beautiful, but its thorns are clearly visible, like the thorns of the rose, a flower which is also sacred to the Virgin. When the thorn is seen beneath the flower, when the beauty of the bloom is protected by the purity of the snow—as in the old English and German carols and legends about the Christmas Rose—then beguilement is conquered, the regime of *Maya* ended, because the true terms of cosmic existence have been unveiled. In the union of Mercy and Rigor, of Beauty (the Flower) and Sobriety (the Winter) embodied by the Virgin (who is *vidya-maya*), the delusive power of ignorance, *avidya-maya*, is definitively overcome.

FOUR

"Tam Lin"—
A Return to the Human Form

The Scottish ballad "Tam Lin" is evidence that the Celtic Pagans too, not just the Christians, recognized the need for the human form to be redeemed from the Regime of Nature. The following version of is the one sung by Sandy Denny and the Fairport Convention, from their classic album *Liege and Lief* [http://www.youtube.com/watch?v=guFZkLxYM6o]:

> I forbid you maidens all
> That wear gold in your hair
> To travel to Carterhaugh
> For young Tam Lin is there.
>
> None that go by Carterhaugh
> But they leave him a pledge
> Either their mantles of green
> Or else their maidenheads.

Janet tied her kirtle green
A bit above her knee
And she's gone to Carterhaugh
As fast as go can she.

She'd not pulled a double rose,
A rose but only two
When up then came young Tam Lin
Says "Lady pull no more".

"And why come you to Carterhaugh
Without command from me?"
"I'll come and go" young Janet said
"And ask no leave of thee".

Janet tied her kirtle green
A bit above her knee
And she's gone to her father
As fast as go can she.

Well up then spoke her father clear
And he spoke meek and mild
"Oh and alas Janet" he said
"I think you go with child."

"Well if that be so" Janet said
"Myself shall bear the blame
There's not a knight in all your hall
Shall get the baby's name.

"For if my love were an earthly knight
As he is an elfin grey
I'd not change my own true love
For any knight you have."

So Janet tied her kirtle green
A bit above her knee
And she's gone to Carterhaugh
As fast as go can she.

"Oh tell to me Tam Lin" she said
"Why came you here to dwell?"
"The Queen of Fairies caught me
When from my horse I fell.

"And at the end of seven years
She pays a tithe to hell
I so fair and full of flesh
And fear'ed be myself.

"But tonight is Halloween
And the fairy folk ride,
Those that would their true love win
At Mile's Cross they must hide.

"First let pass the horses black
And then let pass the brown
Quickly run to the white steed
And pull the rider down.

"For I'll ride on the white steed,
The nearest to the town
For I was an earthly knight,
They give me that renown.

"Oh they will turn me in your arms
To a newt or a snake
But hold me tight and fear not,
I am your baby's father.

"And they will turn me in your arms
Into a lion bold
But hold me tight and fear not
And you will love your child.

"And they will turn me in your arms
Into a naked knight
But cloak me in your mantle
And keep me out of sight".

In the middle of the night
She heard the bridle ring
She heeded what he did say
And young Tam Lin did win.

Then up spoke the Fairy Queen,
An angry Queen was she
"Woe betide her ill-farred face,
An ill death may she die.

"Had I known Tam Lin" she said
"This night I did see
I'd have looked him in the eyes
And turned him to a tree."

"Tam Lin" is a song about the reconciliation of two worlds, the all-too-human world of daily life, and the uncanny realm of Faerie. And the agent of this reconciliation is a female heroine, Janet, who acts as the go-between between two wounded kingdoms, two failures to attain the fullness of the Human Form; the name "Janet" suggests the two-faced god Janus, who looks both ways, toward the human world and toward the Unseen. The lord of the human world, Janet's father, is weak and ineffectual; the knight of Faerie, Tam Lin, is under a spell that has bound him to inhuman powers.

Janet is like a female Orpheus when he made pilgrimage to bring back the soul of his wife Euridice from the underworld, and she is successful where Orpheus failed. She may also be compared to Psyche, who harrowed Hell just as Orpheus did, and who had to thwart the goddess Aphrodite—in Janet's case, the Queen of Faerie—to be reunited to her beloved Eros, Aphrodite's son. Janet boldly enters the Faerie realm and becomes pregnant by the uncanny charmed knight Tam Lin, learns from him how he may be freed from the spell cast upon him by the Queen, and does indeed free him, returning him to the human world—the suggestion being that Tam Lin's spirit has passed into Janet's womb (her "mantle") with his seed, allowing her to bring him to a second birth as a human child. And since she accomplishes this not by visible Divine aid or by respecting any taboo, but by sheer boldness, she must in herself represent an element of Divinity—in this case the principle of true feeling, with all its power to humanize the uncanny elements of the soul—a particularly feminine manifestation of Divine Wisdom. Wisdom gives birth to Certainty, and Certainty does what it must.

Janet's father is human morality devoid of power; Tam Lin is the power of Faerie devoid of both morality and humanity. The human world must be reinfused with the transpersonal force that alone makes human life possible; the lost and uncanny world of Faerie whose Queen is a vassal of Hell—reminding us of the Limbo of

Dante's *Inferno*—must renounce its hold on the human form. And it is precisely human feeling in its transcendental fullness that can accomplish this task. In one rendition of the Eastern Orthodox Icon of St. George slaying the dragon, the dragon is held fast by a Princess so the saint can impale him on his lance; the beast is tied to her waist by a thin red cord. This represents the delicacy of true feeling as the necessary complement to spiritual heroism. And behind the Princess stands a Tower on whose balcony, watching the battle, stand a King and a Prince, with another Princess between them. The Tower symbolizes the human soul, in which Thought (the King) and Will (the Prince) can only be reconciled by Feeling (the Princess). But in a situation where no spiritual Hero appears, where morality is powerless and the uncanniness of the unredeemed passions has appropriated the magical numinosity that is proper only to the Spirit, true feeling—secretly infused by that Spirit—must act on its own, exposing itself to the uncanny powers of Faerie so as to humanize them within its own soul, its own womb. It is only this deed—both exploit and sacrifice—that can redeem those powers and make them fertile for human life.

Now let's take a closer look at the song's symbolism:

> I forbid you maidens all
> That wear gold in your hair
> To travel to Carterhaugh
> For young Tam Lin is there.

Janet's first act is to place Tam Lin off limits to other women (aristocratic women who wear gold in their hair), thus striking a blow against the promiscuity and chaos of subhuman instinct.

> None that go by Carterhaugh
> But they leave him a pledge
> Either their mantles of green
> or else their maidenheads.

Green is the color of life and fertility, the heraldic color of Venus; to surrender one's green mantle is to give up either one's erotic powers or one's life—and if either is lost, Tam Lin can never be saved. But instead Janet surrenders her virginity, and so enters into a dangerous pact with the powers of Faerie.

> She'd not pulled a double rose,
> A rose but only two
> When up then came young Tam Lin
> Says "Lady pull no more".

The two roses are two lovers. If Janet had gone on gathering more roses this would have indicated a fall into promiscuity and psychic dissipation. But she has the virtue of discipline-in-eros; her sights are set on her one and only beloved, not on every faun and satyr in that shady kingdom. She's after Tam Lin and no one else.

> "For if my love were an earthly knight
> As he is an elfin grey
> I'd not change my own true love
> For any knight you have."

According to Ritson's *Fairy Mythology*, 1878, pp. 26–27, "The fairies of the moors were often clad in heath-brown or lichen-dyed garments, whence the epithet of 'Elfin-grey'"—though in our time this name necessarily reminds us of the type of "space alien" known as the Grey, who is undoubtedly a distant relatives of the Elves, being a member of another of the many races who inhabit the Intermediary Plane. Our word "fairy" comes from the Latin "*fata*", one of the Three Fates that the Greeks called the Moirae. Akin but not identical to the Moirae were the Graeae, another Greek triple goddess—three hags who shared one eye and one tooth between them. The Graeae were cousins to the Fates; their name means "The Grey Ones".

> "Oh tell to me Tam Lin" she said
> "Why came you here to dwell?"
> "The Queen of Fairies caught me
> When from my horse I fell.
>
> "And at the end of seven years
> She pays a tithe to hell
> I so fair and full of flesh
> And fear'ed be myself."

Here, as in the ballad of "Thomas Rymer", we see that the realm of Faerie is a kind of ante-chamber to Hell, a province of the Earthly

Paradise now fallen into alienation from the Spirit, precisely because it has been divorced from the fullness of the human form.

> "But tonight is Halloween
> And the fairy folk ride,
> Those that would their true love win
> At Mile's Cross they must hide.
>
> "First let pass the horses black
> And then let pass the brown
> Quickly run to the white steed
> And pull the rider down."

To wait until the black horses and the brown horses have passed is to resist being swept away by the elemental potencies of matter. Only the one who can withstand their attraction will be able to discern the white horse, seed of the Spirit hidden among subhuman passions and powers, and seize its Rider, that aspect of the human form that's been lost through enslavement to the Great Goddess, the Regime of Nature falsely considered as separate from God.

> "For I'll ride on the white steed,
> The nearest to the town
> For I was an earthly knight,
> They give me that renown."

Here we see that even the powers of Faerie grudgingly grant precedence to the human form and the dignity of earthly life; the reason they wish to abduct human beings is because they know (as we have already seen) that only Humanity—in this age at least—bears what the Qur'an calls *the Trust*; Man alone is vice-regent of God in the manifest universe. And if the Fairies (who are the Jinn) ever held this Trust in the distant past—which is debatable—they are now disinherited, and so must make their living as thieves. But whatever of the human soul they are able to steal does not retain the boon that they so covet, the power to humanize them. Their very possession of it has rendered it elvish and uncanny, and so it is of no real use to them; this is the great frustration that the Faerie powers are subject to in the present human age.

"Oh they will turn me in your arms
To a newt or a snake
But hold me tight and fear not,
I am your baby's father.

"And they will turn me in your arms
Into a lion bold
But hold me tight and fear not
And you will love your child.

"And they will turn me in your arms
Into a naked knight
But cloak me in your mantle
And keep me out of sight".

This is the crux of the action. As in the Grimm's fairy tale "The Frog Prince", the power of genuine human feeling, which has its root above in the celestial realms, not below in the world of instinct, can and must endure the uncanniness and degradation of the male principle fallen into the clutches of the elements, always keeping its eye on the human potential within the ever-changing elemental masks, till fallen Man is re-humanized. And this process has three definite stages to it: the *amphibian/reptile* stage, the *mammal* stage, and the *human* stage, reminding us of the theory that the human being possess three distinct brains: the *reptile* brain (the brain-stem and cerebellum), the *mammal* brain (the limbic system), and the *new* brain (the neo-cortex), the one that expresses our essential humanity. But the newly-regained human form must not be immediately exposed again to the Faerie powers lest it be once more abducted and lost; it must be "cloistered" within the heart of Janet until she is completely reintegrated into the human world. She must exhibit the virtue of contemplative discretion and not "throw her pearls before swine", since to reveal a spiritual potential before its time is to abort it. Only after the gestation period established by Providence is complete can she give birth to it not as an uncanny changeling, but as a fully human child.

In the middle of the night
She heard the bridle ring
She heeded what he did say
And young Tam Lin did win.

Then up spoke the Fairy Queen,
An angry Queen was she
"Woe betide her ill-farred face,
An ill death may she die.

"Had I known Tam Lin" she said
"This night I did see
I'd have looked him in the eyes
And turned him to a tree."

Here we can see the fundamental antipathy between the Realm of Faerie and the human world. If it were not for the race of men, the Queen of Faerie would truly be the Great Goddess, the principle of all that exists. But the existence of humanity insultingly relativizes and demotes her by revealing the existence of a Celestial Realm that only Humanity possesses the key to; the one and only road to that Realm passes straight through the Human Form. The Queen can now only hurl ineffectual curses and wish that she had turned Tam Lin to a tree when she had the chance. And what kind of tree? A tree rooted in earth, undoubtedly. But the Human Form is in one sense a tree already, a tree rooted not in the earth but in the sky. As possessor of the Trust he is the stem of universal manifestation—the Tree of Life itself.

FIVE

"The Cherry-Tree Carol"—
Knowledge is a Gift, Not an Acquisition

The "Cherry-Tree Carol" is one of the Child Ballads, number 54 to be exact. It is said to be based on an account of Jesus' infancy that appears in Chapter XX of *The Gospel of Pseudo-Matthew*, which was probably written between AD 600 and 625, and which bears some resemblance to a similar story told of the Virgin Mary and a date-palm, not a cherry-tree, in *Mary*, the 19th *surah* of the Qur'an, verses 23ff. Since this *surah* is believed to have been received by the Prophet Muhammad shortly before June in the year 622, the date of his *Hijra* from Mecca to Yathrib, it could conceivably have been the source for the story of Mary and the cherry-tree in *Pseudo-Matthew*—though some of course will say that the story must have passed in the opposite direction. A version of this carol—really more of a ballad—was sung by Jean Ritchie, but my favorite is still the one by Joan Baez, which is simple, compact, highly poetic, and sufficient to my theme. It goes like this:

> When Joseph was an old man
> An old man was he,
> He married Virgin Mary
> The Queen of Galilee.
>
> Joseph and Mary
> Walked through an orchard green;
> There were berries and cherries
> As thick as might be seen.
>
> And Mary spoke to Joseph
> So meek and so mild:
> "Gather me some cherries,
> For I am with child."
>
> And Joseph flew in anger
> In anger flew he,
> "Let the Father of the Baby
> Gather cherries for thee!"
>
> Then up spoke Baby Jesus
> From within Mary's womb:
> "Bend down the tallest tree
> That my mother might have some."
>
> And bent down the tallest branch
> Till it touched Mary's hand
> Cried she, "O look thou Joseph,
> I have cherries by command."

The literal meaning and sentiment of this carol conceals an inner significance which is the exact reverse of what appears on the surface. Among Christian saints, Joseph has the dubious distinction of having (so to speak) been "cuckolded by God", chosen to raise a child not his own, the child of a bride much younger than he and one who necessarily appeared, to faithless and worldly eyes, as guilty of adultery. (Certain commentaries to the Jewish *Talmud* shamelessly exploit this slander to the fullest possible extent.) The

Gospels themselves tell us that Joseph was deeply disturbed by his wife's pregnancy, till an angel of God appeared and revealed to him that Mary's condition was the result of her being overshadowed by the Holy Spirit. Thus the shame of Joseph in the eyes of the world concealed, and also protected, a pre-eminence that places him second to Mary alone in the annals of Christian sanctity.

The anger expressed by Joseph in "The Cherry-Tree Carol" is obviously anger at the apparent revelation of his wife's adultery; this, however, is not the only perspective from which the matter can be viewed. Joseph refuses to gather cherries to satisfy his pregnant wife's food cravings; instead, he bitterly and ironically challenges the father of the baby to perform that task—a challenge immediately responded to by the unborn child himself. If, as Jesus said in the Gospel of John, "I and the Father are One"; if He in fact represents God's Self-conception within the womb of the purest of the human race, herself conceived without sin; then the Father of the Baby did indeed gather cherries for the Virgin, who was in effect both His wife and His mother. But what does it mean that Joseph would not, or could not, gather this fruit for Mary himself, that only the Holy Word within her had the right to perform that task?

If we take the cherries as a symbol of the gifts of God, the fruits of Divine Grace, then the answer becomes clear. For Mary to ask Joseph to gather cherries for her shows that she still bore a trace within her of the *curiosity* of Eve that led her to eat of the Tree of the Knowledge of Good and Evil. She is essentially asking Joseph, as a human being, to gather the fruits of Divine Knowledge for her on his own initiative, by his own self-will—a self-will that is, or would be if he were to give in to her demands, enslaved and dominated by her merely human concupiscence. But Joseph, as God's chosen guardian of Mary's Virginity, instead asserts his own dominance, his righteous, masculine and protective authority, by which he tells her in effect: "If I were to give in to your pleading it would be a violation of your Virginity, of which the cherry is of course the emblem; only God has the right and the power to gather the Fruit of Knowledge for you—*carnal* Knowledge included—while still keeping your Virginity intact." How different from the meek and self-effacing Platonic husband, whose wife is a great Queen without his ever having the privilege of being her king, is this unbending and righteous guardian of the great Holiness placed in his charge! This is the sort of strength we need if we are to protect the receptive integrity of the Wisdom within us.

Divine Knowledge is not to be gathered by human will acting under the command of human curiosity; this is the very transgression that led to the Fall of Man. But Mary was the chosen recipient of the One destined to reverse, redress and obliterate that Fall. It was her Virginity itself, a Virginity that could accept Knowledge only as a gift of God, not as a shiny plaything to be grasped in greed or envy or lust, and possessed in pride, that allowed Truth Himself to be *conceived* within her. And Joseph, her husband, was the delegated guardian of that Virginity, a simple craftsman who knew nothing of the secrets of the Spirit, nor hankered for nor ever expected to grasp anything so exalted—until an Angel appeared to him in a dream on three separate occasions, carrying the commands of his Lord: first, in order to unveil the secret of the Annunciation; second, in order to warn of the hatred of the World; third, in order to reveal that this World had now lost its power. The *sacrificium intellectus* ("sacrifice of the intellect") spoken of by St. Ignatius Loyola and other Christian writers is thus not a rejection of the gift of Divine Knowledge— as if Mary were to have spurned the cherries that were attracted to her and offered to her directly by the God within her—but a rejection of all *possessiveness* in the realm of the intellect, in the understanding that, as the Sufis say, spiritual states—the only channels through which Divine Knowledge can come to us—are gifts of God, not acquisitions of human labor. Nor can curiosity—the sort of curiosity through which the Serpent tempted Eve in the Garden— receive such Knowledge; only the submissive willingness *never to demand that Divine Secrets be revealed* is willing and able to truly know; in the words of the Virgin Mary herself from the Gospel of Luke, "Let it be done unto me according to Thy Word."

SIX

"Farewell, Farewell"—
The Call of Hyperborea

The song "Farewell, Farewell", by Richard Thompson, late of the folk-rock band Fairport Convention, has affinities with the traditional ballad "Will O'Willoby" or "Willie O'Winsbury"; nonetheless it remains what used to be called a "literary ballad", meaning a ballad composed by a known poet, not by some singing but unsung artist of the "anonymous folk". (You can hear it at https://www.youtube.com/watch?v=69sLI4n674s.) And since Mr. Thompson is still alive and kicking, I am at serious risk of being told, upon publishing this exegesis, "That's not what I meant at all, mate, yer whistling in the wind." I might only reply, most humbly and circumspectly, that living artists working in deep folk traditions may become host to the knowledge of the dead, often without they themselves realizing it or at least being clear on what exactly they are transmitting—as when Jean Ritchie informed me that she supplied a missing stanza of her "Fair Nottamun Town" based on a vision she had while walking in the woods. It was a vision of a procession of figures arranged according to a precise Hermetic/Alchemical symbolism, a symbolism which meant nothing to her beyond its mysterious, evocative, "poetic" power since she had never studied Hermeticism or Alchemy, nor was she in any way interested in them. (Lots of musicians are like that: they insist that a song means what it *is*, not what some academic or occult interloper might read into it. My reply has always been, "I'm not reading things *into* it, but *out* of it.")

"Farewell, Farewell" takes the form of a dialogue between an exiled or deceased father and his living sons:

[THE VOICE OF THE FATHER]

"Farewell, farewell to you who would hear
You lonely travelers all
The cold north wind will blow again
The winding road does call."

[THE VOICE OF THE SONS,
THE VOICE OF THE FATHER]

"And will you never return to see
Your bruised and beaten sons?"
"Oh, I would, I would, if welcome I were
For they love me, every one."

[THE VOICE OF THE SONS]

"And will you never cut the cloth
Or drink the light to be?
And can you never swear a year
To any one of we?"

[THE VOICE OF THE FATHER]

"No, I will never cut the cloth
Or drink the light to be
But I'll swear a year to one who lies
Asleep along side of me.

"Farewell, farewell to you who would hear
You lonely travelers all
The cold north wind will blow again
The winding road does call."

The Father has died and gone to the next world; the principle of spiritual Guidance is now hidden behind the door of death. And so the sons lament. (This song could well have been written by the followers of a great spiritual Master after his passing.)

"Cut the cloth and drink the light to be" could refer to the initiatory rites of the particular esoteric school the dead teacher guided, possibly (given the song's British provenance) a school of Christian Hermeticism. "Drink the light to be" might suggest some ritual that symbolized and foreshadowed the final goal of the Path, maybe a shared cup of wine or some more powerful intoxicant. As for "cut the cloth", this could indicate an "investiture" with a sacred initiatory robe or a piece of cloth with a similar significance—perhaps a symbolic funeral shroud as is used in the initiation rites of certain Sufi orders, indicating "death to the self", or the apron or similar piece of cloth conferred upon the initiate in Freemasonry or in the *futuwwah* (chivalric) brotherhoods of the Muslim world. The meaning of this verse is that the dead master cannot initiate us from the other world; for that a living master is needed. But we can still receive a helpful spiritual influence from him—possibly in the dream state—if we are willing, as it were, to *sleep on his grave*, to die spiritually to the world as he has died to it in both body and soul.

But what is it for the father to "swear a year" to one of his sons? It came to me (somehow) that this might refer to a lordly or royal custom, perhaps universal at one time in the Indo-European world, of the king who chooses to retire in his old age instead of waiting for death to overtake him, thereby dedicating himself (like the Persian *kalendars* or perpetually wandering dervishes) to a "peripatetic" life of constant pilgrimage until death, accepting each year the hospitality of a different one of his children. In doing so he would return, as the Persians might say, from *Iran* to *Turan*, from sedentary city life to the primordial purity of the nomad, abandoning the life of Cain, the first murderer who founded the first city, for the life of Abel the nomadic herdsman, who was "too good for this world." We can possibly see the degenerated remnants of such a custom in Shakespeare's *King Lear*, where the old king retires in the foolish expectation of being sheltered and maintained by his three daughters, one after the other. This retirement would of course have had a spiritual significance; it would have been an initiation into the final *ashrama* or stage of life, that of the wandering wise man; in the *I Ching* the same transition is represented by the motion from the fifth line of a given hexagram, that of the Ruler, to the sixth and last line, that of the Sage. And we can still barely make out the lineaments of this role and function behind the tragedy of Lear's exile. His madness is in one sense a symbol of death to the world and the attainment of a "crazy" wisdom, all foolishness to the "wise of this world", that transcends the *dharma* of kings, their duty of rational insight coupled with courageous and principled action. In the present song the deceased Master may be compared to a king who has retired from the world, but who may yet visit his sons to impart the kind of wisdom this world can never understand. Such wandering sages would have functioned, in the words of Lear himself, as "God's spies".

The North is the direction of Hyperborea, the Polar Paradise, the gate to which is the North Star, the "still point of the turning world" in T. S. Eliot's phrase, the visible point of eternity in the temporal order. The South is the point of the natural order and the "natural man", the place named by W. B. Yeats, in his poem "Byzantium", "That dolphin-torn, that gong-tormented sea." The West is the point of natural death, the destination of all who pass from this world uninitiated. But the North is the point of *initiatory* death: "I call it death-in-life and life-in death", said Yeats in the same poem. It is the hard road of purgation, the goal of all who have "died before they die", of those travelers who fight upstream, like the spawning salmon, against the full force of the North Wind, that ascetic spiritual power that pacifies the passions and makes the soul ready for Hyperborea, the land of eternal Springtime behind the North Wind. Dante, in his *Divine Comedy*, places the northern constellations of the Bears above the Terrestrial Paradise at the summit of the Mount of Purgatory, which represents the spiritual Path.

In almost every symbolic system of the four directions, the whole world over, the North is a point of rigor; the Lakota call it the direction of purification where the White Giant lives. But in many systems it is simply regarded as the region of demonic evil. This is partly due to the fact that, in our own age at least, no one can lawfully take the Northern road who has not first completed the Eastern mysteries of revelation and salvation: the free gift of God, to a benighted humanity, of salvation and light. Whoever—like so many self-styled "esoterists"—essays the North while despising the East, the point from which the sacred norms of the God-given revealed religions come to us, will slip, like Lear did, into the sin of *hubris*, and enact a titanic inflation and fall.

But the North is rigorous in any case. The northern or polar point represents the Zenith, which you can only reach by struggling against the entire gravity of existence. To die before you die is to shed the five skins of manifest existence that the Hindus call the *koshas*, and thereby rise up the ladder of the seven *chakras*, the "winding road" represented by the hermetic *caduceus*, until you reach the Crown.

On a more outer level, this song suggests the lament of the persecuted true sons of a King or Lord whose place has been usurped by a false power—which, in terms of Britain, could well represent the

93

plight of persecuted Catholics, perhaps as seen from the perspective of a specific Christian Hermetic school, after Henry VIII usurped the powers of the Roman hierarchy and bombarded and closed the monasteries, including the Abbey at Glastonbury—an event that Blake covertly lamented in his prologue to *The Marriage of Heaven and Hell*. In a specifically Christian context, the Lord who has passed on, whose sons still long for his return, and who asks them to make room for that return by participating in his death, would be a reflection of Christ the King.

9

The Poetic Art in the 21st Century: a Rant

for Ed McClanahan

Jack Spicer said: "I can't stand to see them
Shimmering in the impossible music
Of the Star Spangled Banner. No one
Accepts this system better than poets,
Their hurts healed for a few dollars."

Well, they are still shimmering,
Only the music is now the music of
Timothy Leary, Jim Morrison,
Frank Zappa and the Merry Pranksters—
The Embalmed Sixties presented to you
Courtesy of the CIA's MK-ULTRA
    mind-control program,
(Which is where LSD came from in the first
    place),
And the National Endowment for the Arts.

Bohemia had some use and rationale
When it was a real alternative to the
    "plastic people" of the 1950's,
To a society dominated by the strait-laced
    bourgeoisie—
But now Bohemia, or what's left of it,
Is pure Establishment, and the middle class
Is dead. You can no longer run away and
    join the hippies
So society and your parents won't bury you
    alive,
And you can't even "go straight" any more,
Can't even clean up your act, get a life,

95

Get married, have children, become a self-
    respecting "productive member of society",
Now that the family has been outlawed
    economically,
And human decency outlawed culturally,
And any way out of the universal Skinner
    Box of the Engineered Society
Either permanently shut down or por-
    trayed as some kind of fanaticism or
    extremism—*religion*, for example—
Leaving us nothing but the Brave New World
    with its licensed deceptions,
Among which is "literature and the arts",
Reduced to a category of acceptable entertainment,
With poetry just another vaudeville act,
Along with juggling, burlesque and standup
    comedy,
Nothing but pure *diversion*, one more necessary
    distraction
From the intolerable truth of our lives and our
    condition.
In the standard establishment poetry of today
The sublime is outlawed,
Depth of feeling swiftly neutralized,
And if anybody is foolhardy enough to approach
    the world of *meaning*—
Well *that* guy gets his name put on a list.
The conventional verse of our time
Takes despair as axiomatic, and then proceeds
To make a little aesthetic space to live in,
Or at least peek into,
On the plains of that despair.
We are all doomed, says 21st Century American
    Poetry,
All headed for death,
Our freedoms stolen,
The planet shot,
But still we can share the little commonalities
    of our daily experience
With others equally doomed, smiling ruefully

at each other through the haze;
Sometimes rising to wit (as long as it's not
   too pointedly intelligent);
Sometimes dipping into nostalgia (as long as
   it never gets deep enough to confront us
   with the depth of our loss—
No orgiastic lamentations, now, or we'll be
   forced to call security—)
That's what my art has been reduced to,
The art that produced Homer and Dante,
And Blake and Shakespeare,
And Whitman and Emily Dickinson,
Now risen to the modest, latter day heights
   of Garrison Keillor,
Who really is the best of them, now,
In the lurid crepuscular twilight of the latter
   days,
The world ending with a bang all around us,
   in the streets outside,
While we, huddled around the flickering firelight
   of the TV screen and the computer monitor
Listen to the same world ending with a whimper,
Courtesy of art and literature, including 21st
   Century Poetry,
And us whimpering along with it, in dull and
   somnolent unison,
As we stare our tasteful uselessness in the face,
A rhythmic, studied uselessness, faithful to the
   subtle textures, stinks and fragrances
Of *language, language* (Ginsberg from "Wichita
   Vortex Sutra"),
Product of our perfect, unconscious and
   intrinsic obedience to society's norms,
Among which must be included the pose of
   youthful rebellion pickled in formaldehyde,
All adding up to the sort of resumé one might
   circulate in hopes of landing the position
Of euthanasia tech, with a letter of rec.,
From the late Dr. Kevorkian
And another from new the poet laureate of the
   coming season…

And the *alternative*? What if there isn't any?
What if all of us are now reduced to what
   even Spicer had to admit when he said,
"Should I throw rocks at them/
To make their naked private bodies bleed?/
No, let them sleep."
But we are not "them", the audience who asks
   only that we pack their sleep with cushions
   plush enough not to wake them,
And decorate with minimalist canvasses or
   nostalgic country scenes
The anteroom of death—*no*. We are those
   who have essayed to *speak*, and so bear
   the responsibility, as Lew Welch put it,
Of becoming the kind of people who might
   have something worth listening to.
But exactly how is this to be done? you ask.
Is it possible? Will it hurt? It won't end up
   being *unhip* will it, heaven forbid?
In answer, all I can do is list the steps:
   1) Wake up and realize that you're in the box.
   2) See if you can conceive, somehow, of a
desire to get *out* of the box.
   3) Try to *imagine* (something poets used to
be able to do in the olden days, or so I am told)
what might *already be there* outside the box,
calling to you, gesturing frantically at you
   through the smoke,
Pounding on your door.
Beyond that, my only advice is:

   American poets, learn your job;
   Write whatever irks the mob;
   Stomp these wimps who fear to *mean*,
   Whose sole craft is to make the scene.
   Born yesterday, to the world they go;
   "Born again" they'll never know.

      Cast a slim eye
      On dusk, on dawn;
      Driver—drive on.

✍ 10 ✍

Lew Welch as Teacher

This essay, minus the Addendum, appeared in The Wars of Love and Other Poems, Sophia Perennis, 2011

LEW WELCH was both my poetic mentor and my first real teacher. But since he was also an alcoholic suicide, it was inevitable that I would have to separate his teaching into negative and positive aspects, the first to be rejected, the second to be accepted with gratitude. Part One of this essay has to do with the first kind of teaching, Part Two with the second.

I: Buzzard Cult, Adieu

My initiator into the art of poetry was Lew Welch. I learned many things of value from him, including some real metaphysical insights that I will deal with below, but his best lesson was negative: "Kid, don't end up like me."

In an attempt to "initiate" me, Lew introduced me to two people who had everything to do with my future spiritual development: Samuel Lewis ("Sufi Sam"), and Carlos Castaneda. Sufi Sam, a kind of bridge figure between the hippies and the world of real Sufi initiation, foreshadowed my entrance into the path of *Tasawwuf*, while Castaneda was a lurid omen of my future magic-dabbling, and my lifelong oversensitivity to dark psychic forces.

Lew, like many poets of the Beat/Hippy era, sometimes thought of himself as a magician—and undoubtedly his most successful magic act was to conjure up a posthumous cult for himself, so as to mystify and glamorize what was, after all, just one more sordid alcoholic suicide.

He did this through a poem entitled "Song of the Turkey Buzzard", which was his suicide note. In an attempt to invent something on the order of "American koans," Lew had composed three riddles: "The Riddle of Bowing", "The Riddle of Hands", and "The Rider Riddle". "The Rider Riddle", which is basically a way of finding one's helping spirit in the form of a "totem" animal or plant, goes like this:

> If you spend as much time on the Mountain as you
> should, she will always give you a Sentient Being to ride:
> animal, plant, insect, reptile, or any of the Numberless Forms:

> What do *you* ride?

> (There is one right answer for every person, and only
> that person can really know what it is.)

"The Mountain" is Mt. Tamalpais in Marin County, California. Lew asked this riddle of himself, and got "turkey buzzard" for an answer. In "Song of the Turkey Buzzard", he says:

> The rider riddle is easy to ask
> But the answer might surprise you.

> How desperately I wanted Cougar
> (I, Leo, etc.)
> brilliant proofs: terrain,
> color, food, all
> nonsense. All made up.

> *They were always there, the*
> *laziest high-fliers, bronze-winged,*
> *the silent ones.*

> . . . .

> They smell sweet
> meat is dry on their talons

> The very opposite of
> death

> bird of re-birth
> buzzard

> meat is rotten meat made
> sweet again....

Lew Welch as Teacher

. . . .

Hear my last Will & Testament:

Among my friends there shall always be
one with proper instructions
for my continuance.

> *Let no one grieve.*
> *I shall have used it all up*
> *used up every bit of it.*
> *What an extravagance!*
> *What a relief!*

On a marked rock, following his orders,
place my meat.

> *All care must be taken not to*
> *frighten the natives of this*
> *barbarous land, who*
> *will not let us die, even*
> *as we wish.*

With proper ceremony disembowel what I
no longer need, that it might more quickly
rot and tempt

my new form

So the buzzards will eat Lew's guts and that's how he will be "rein-carnated" as a Buzzard God. No personal immortality, not even any "spiritual" reincarnation, and certainly no *moksha*, no Perfect Total Enlightenment. Lew meat will become buzzard meat, and that's that. And note the flattering, wily come-on to his "successor": The *one* with proper instructions for the continuance of Lewis Barrett Welch is—why *me*, of course!

Never once (though Buzzard was Milarepa's totem bird) did I hear a word from Lew about Nirvana, the Dharmakaya, God, the Great Spirit, Brahman, the Tao, Allah, the Atman, or any other ren-dition of Absolute Truth. Like others of his generation he was inter-ested in a kind of secularized, "tricksterish" Buddhism—the "Beat Zen" of Alan Watts—but hardly a word about Nirvana or Perfect Total Enlightenment as a state of Liberation in Absolute Reality.

Well, maybe there are too many words on that subject already, too many words and not enough practice. But it's also possible that Lew basically shared Gary Snyder's view of Buddhism, which I heard from him on the occasion of Philip Whalen's memorial service at Green Gulch Zen Center: "Face it, Charles—Buddhism is *atheism*."

The only moment of simple religious piety—that all-important Step One—in all of Lew's poetry is the following, entitled *He Asks for Guidance*:

> Avalokiteshvara, Buddha of Compassion, Original
> Bodhisattva, who spoke the Prajñaparamita Sutra
>   of the heart,
> Kannon in Japan, Kuan-Yin in China, Chenrezig in
> Tibet, no God, but guide, O
> countless thousands of returning men and women
> of every place and time,
> as Virgil for Dante, through Dante's Hell,
> please guide me through Samsara.

Lew might have known more than he said; he certainly *was* more than he said, as we all are—but note this: It's not "please *liberate* me from Samsara," but "please *guide me through* Samsara." Well, in a way that's a modest, honest request, a realistically muted expectation. But if Avalokiteshvara is not a living symbol of Absolute Reality in the guise of Perfect Total Enlightenment—and in Lew's rendition of him, we are not really sure he is—then whence his power to guide? And if Lew could not believe in Absolute Reality, then how could be become available to that guidance? It was Beatrice who sent Virgil, and St. Lucy who sent Beatrice, and the Blessed Virgin who sent St. Lucy, and the Will of God working through the Blessed Virgin. But who or what sent Lew's Avalokiteshvara? Alavokiteshvara is the emanation of the Dharmakaya, the Original Mind, the Clear Light of the Void. Lew Welch's grasp on this truth, however, was unsteady. After Hell comes the *Purgatorio*, and the *Paradiso* after that; would that Lew could have seen, and named, the whole Path that stretched before him.

Lew Welch was in many ways a materialist. He usually scorned Christianity: "Who could ever worship a *Holy Ghost*?"—though he once said to me (I was basically in my Blakean Christian period then), "Maybe Jesus really is your Master." And it was this material-istic nature-worship—essentially the "paganism" of Sir James Frazer and Robert Graves (the two books he told me every poet should read were *The Golden Bough* and *The White Goddess*)—that replaced for him any kind of, effective, serious Buddhism, which would have started him out with certain basic behavioral requirements, like "no booze." And so he fell back, at least partly, on a simple, literal wor-ship of the earth and sun:

> Here comes the sun. It's the only god we've got. It's shining on the earth. It [the earth] is our mother. It is a big round ball [from *How I Work as a Poet*].

So how does a materialist conceive of immortality—apart, that is, from the ministrations of cryogenics and genetic engineering? Lew's way was to opt for what is called "poetic immortality," which is essentially *immortality in the memory of the living*. But he went a step further. I believe that Lew Welch also wanted to be *held in a stable form and a conscious state after death* by that same memory. That's why he founded his Buzzard Cult. He wanted to trap and hold the attention of others after his death so as to maintain his identity—something he undoubtedly also did during life. When the Mexicans, on the Day of the Dead, put tortillas and tequila on the graves of the departed, they are doing the same thing. They are trying to keep the dead "alive" as ghosts—well-fed ghosts who will hopefully be satis-fied enough not to vampirize the living. Lew, however, may ulti-mately have been unable to avoid the vampire trip, as witness at least two copycat suicides I certainly know of, those of Jack Boyce—an "accidental" death that was undoubtedly suicidal in intent—and "Burl," a sleepy, sodden youth who attached himself to Lew's wife Magda after Lew disappeared. But what is kept "alive" by the psychic energy of the living is not the actual spirit of the departed, but only the ghostly residue of the unredeemed psyche—in other words, the *ego:* the original vampire. In the words of W.B. Yeats, from "All Souls' Night", Lew ultimately wanted to be one who had

> ...a ghost's right
> His element is so fine
> Being sharpened by his death

103

To drink from the wine-breath
While our gross palates drink from the whole wine.

That *is* a pretty classy-sounding afterlife—until you actually get
there and see what it's like. The narcissist sacrifices his living flesh
and spirit to the vampire of his self-image. "We invent ourselves,"
wrote Lew in "The Entire Sermon by the Red Monk", "out of ingre-
dients we didn't choose, by a process we can't control.... All you
really say [supreme irony!] is 'Love me for myself alone'.... It is also
possible to *uninvent* yourself. By a process you can't control. But
you invented Leo. Forget it." Lew, in this poem, defines his poetic
persona, "Leo," as the product of a *successful* act of narcissism—as if
there could be such a thing—and explicitly rejects the spiritual
Path: *the path of self-uninvention.* But no act of narcissism can really
be "successful," simply because narcissism is a living hell. Gleaming
in the reflected light of your own radiant image in the pool, you
trap and lock the attention of everyone around you. But none of
that attention really *gets* to you. All the love and admiration and
compassion and help you so desperately (and silently) crave is
attracted to and eaten by that endlessly talking image, leaving the
real you starving: this is the *oral hell* the Buddhists reserve for those
they call the *pretas,* the "hungry ghosts." Lew was capable of making
many people love him, but could receive love from no-one. He let
himself starve all his life for the love that might have saved him,
because it would have destroyed his glorious self-image, his "Leo."
He even claimed to have made the youngest suicide-attempt on
record, by going on a hunger-strike while still on the bottle—and
(ironically) the bottle was the one thing he never got off of. Lew had
so deeply despaired of the love he needed that he was finally willing
to sacrifice himself to the self-image he *thought* was actually getting
it—and if he had to live through a quasi-eternity as a Buzzard God,
he figured that was a small price to pay for *the food.* An image on a
TV screen cannot receive love, however, and all who give their love
to such subhuman images are signing up for an extended stay in
Xbalbá, the Castle of the Vampires.

And the saddest thing is, so many of us (including myself)
"bought" the Buzzard Cult. Whenever we'd see a turkey buzzard sail
over, we'd say, "there goes Lew." The Buzzard Cult allowed us to

deny *everything*: that Lew, by his suicide, had demonstrated at least some pretty serious flaws in his spiritual life; that all those glamorous bohemian death-trips were nothing but simple despair after all; that we too needed love, and to give love, but had despaired of ever finding it, given up on it so long ago we couldn't even remember it, despite all the counterculture propaganda of the Beatles and so many others, their wan, pastel mewing about "love is all you need". (It wasn't love we were singing about, it was only sex . . . and ultimately it wasn't even sex we were singing about, it was only pornography, only *images*—"sexual" or "spiritual" as you will.) Lew trained us to seek inflated glamour instead of true love—love, of course, being "romantic", "unhip", something requiring some level of basic humility, some modicum of genuine, sincere, unglamorous humanity. How Philistine! How bourgeois! How beneath the Pride of the Lion! And how bleak and terrible the forboding, in the craw of the glamour-addict, of the withdrawal to come, the terminal deadness of reality without all that psychic glamour to keep it hopping. (To endure that deadness, that "dry drunk", without looking away, like "the salt of the earth", is the sole key to the renewal of life—that, and a basic faith in God, an understanding that Reality, in Lew's words, "goes on whether I look at it or not." In Shakespeare's *The Merchant of Venice*, the portrait of Portia is found in the leaden casket, not in the gold or silver ones. Only lead—found, accepted, and lived with—can be transmuted into the Alchemical Gold.)

In his book *Axe Handles*, Gary Snyder has a poem entitled "For/ From Lew":

> Lew Welch just turned up one day,
> Live as you and me. "Damn, Lew" I said,
> "you didn't shoot yourself after all."
> "Yes I did" he said,
> and even then I felt the tingling down my back.
> "Yes you did, too—I can feel it now."
> "Yeah," he said,
> "There's a basic fear between your world and
> mine. I don't know why.
> What I came to say, was,
> Teach the children about the cycles.

The life cycles. All the other cycles.
That's what it's all about, and it's all forgot."

I've always had the impression that this poem must have been based on a dream that Gary had. Around the time it was probably written, and certainly before I read it, I also had a dream about Lew, which resulted in the following poem; the last four lines of it were dictated, word for word, in the dream itself:

I saw the Sun set up in the distance, like a temple on a plain
Animals crashing through forests inside its face.
And my dead teacher, seated, on the orbit of the Earth,
Musing on his old love the Earth and Sun,
And allowing himself, sadly,
To forget it.

This is the age when all stories have been told
The dead going on without poetry,
And poetry telling them the
Truth of gravity's art.

I believe that these two poems are parts of the same "message" from Lew. For him to be sitting on the orbit of the earth in my dream is also a reference to "cycles," but with a different twist—more like the Buddhist "wheel of existence" that the Buddhas no longer turn on because they are now sitting at the center of it, "the still point of the turning world" (T. S. Eliot from the *Four Quartets*).

In another vision I had of Lew after his death, he said to me: "Things don't change here as fast as I thought they would." This is the wages of the Buzzard Cult. He thought our attention to him after his death would save him, but all it did (maybe, maybe) was imprison him. If so, we'd better do what we can to turn him loose—and holding on to a false, idealistic memory of a "great teacher" when we should be praying for the liberation of a despairing soul in torment is definitely not the way to do it. Lew *was* a great teacher in many ways—but if we're ever going to *matriculate*, we will have to confront his last, and toughest, lesson.

So I hereby declare the Buzzard Cult officially dissolved, before everybody who ever heard of it passes from this world. It was a kind of drug, designed by Lew and all the rest of us, to sedate us against the unbearable tragedy of those times. When it comes to the turkey buzzard drug, I for one am going cold turkey.

II: Freedom from the World of Words

It is common to hear people say things like: "Poetry (or whatever other art) is my spiritual Path." However, people like Plato, or Ramana Maharshi, or Muhammad, or Jalaluddin Rumi, who actually functioned as guides on the spiritual Path, were extremely wary of poetry. Plato, in the Republic, called poets "liars"; Ramana Maharshi discouraged the composition of poetry because it diverts spiritual potential away from Liberation and toward self-expression; and the Prophet Muhammad (peace and blessings be upon him), in the *surah* of the Qur'an called "The Poets", heard straight from God that poets can best be described as those who *say that which they do not*. And Rumi called poetry "tripe". Be that as it may, can poetry still be a spiritual Path in some way, or at least part of one?

The basic problem with poetry, in spiritual terms, is that it falsely suggests to us that to be a poet is to be a *creator*, that the world called into being by the poetic art is in some sense a real world. But the truth is, only God creates. To believe anything else, to believe that the human being as poet, or as technologist, or as political leader is in some sense a co-creator in partnership with God, is heresy, and blasphemy—by which I mean that it is simply not true. Everything has already been created by God, from all eternity; man, apart from God, can create nothing. The ego, however, will never accept this. It begins by seeing itself as a co-creator with God, and ends by taking itself to *be* God. Instead of understanding all things as words spoken by God, first in eternity and then in time, it forgets that it has first *heard* these words, and only later learned how to speak them. It forgets that "In the beginning was the word, and the word was with God, and the word was God." Thus we can say that the poet is the very image of the ego's foolish self-deification, and all the disastrous consequences that go with it.

Still, whether we are poets or not, we are now fallen—fallen into the world of words. We do not see reality; we do not live in a real world. We inhabit a phony world "created" by our obsessive, unconscious, verbal definitions of things, the kingdom of the monkey-mind. And given that this false, delusive, beguiling and terrifying world is produced by our *unconsciousness* of the effects of human language on our perception of things, only a complete *consciousness* of those effects can free us from that world, that *samsara*; like William Burroughs once said, "Communication must be made conscious and total: that's the only way to stop it." And who, at least in potential, are more conscious of the effects and qualities of human language than the poets? Nonetheless, we will never become conscious enough of what human language is and how it operates on us simply by *talking*; we also need to learn, in the words of Lew Welch from his poem "Wobbly Rock", how "to sit real still and keep your mouth shut." (Wobbly Rock, as Lew says in the poem itself, is "a real rock ... resting on actual sand at the surf's edge:/Muir Beach, California. ... Size of the largest haystack/It moves when hit by waves/Actually shudders." Lew used to sit on that rock to meditate; it has a precisely square little step or cleft on it that makes a perfect meditation seat [half lotus]. I've meditated there myself. If Rome is the Seat or See of Peter, Wobbly Rock was the See of Lew.)

The French word *trouvère* and the Provençal *troubadour* mean "finder"; the Greek word *poetes* means "maker". If we think that we, as speakers, are makers first and finders only second, then we are deluded. Only God is the First Speaker; we are *finders* first, finders of the First Words of God spoken in Eternity; only later are we makers. We work exclusively on what has already been given, and—if we are true makers, not chaotic babblers—only *according* to what has already been given. If we want to take the audacious and dangerous step of speaking human words, we will have to learn how to *listen* first—and to hear is to obey.

One thing Lew Welch tried to teach was how to squeeze many meanings into a few words, a skill which is related to the opposite, *hermeneutic* ability to unpack those meanings, to unfold them, expand them, bring them to light. This reciprocity between synthesis and analysis, between composition and exegesis, puts us in touch with the alternation of the seasons, with the birth and death of animals and human beings, and ultimately with the creation and destruction of the universe. It teaches us that God is always and hiding from us in the act of showing Himself, and showing Himself in the act of self-concealment; He is always creating the universe by composing it, and then destroying it by revealing the inner meaning of what was composed. As Lew said, posthumously, in Gary Snyder's poem *"For/From Lew"*: "Teach the children about the cycles/ The life cycles, all the other cycles./ That's what it's all about/ And it's all forgot."

Lew's deepest and densest attempt to pack the most lore into the fewest words is his poem "Doctor, Can You Spell Nebuchadnezzar Without Any Z?"* (*Overheard from the mouth of a senile old Irish lady on her deathbed.):

A turf and a clod spells "Nebuchad"

A knife and a razor spells "Nebuchadnezzar"

Two silver spoons and a gold ring
Spells Nebuchadnezzar, the King.

My first impression of this poem was, "Nice, extremely pleasurable, it has density, it's tasty, I can chew it. But it's slight, it's just word-play, it's only melody." Somehow, though, it unconsciously engaged my understanding, till I came up with a deeper interpretation: *A turf and a clod*: The grave. *A knife and a razor*: Surgery (razor to shave the skin, scalpel to cut it). *Two silver spoons and a gold ring*: A hard marriage, two doted-on children, all finally wearing her out. The title: Two ideas of death intersecting in delirium—the last letter of the alphabet representing death, and Nebuchadnezzar as King Death, to whom she is espoused. She asks the doctor if she can escape death by a spell, or re-spelling, of her fate. The poem's answer is: "No". And note how time flows backwards: Death, surgery, childbirth, marriage. This is what the Tibetans call "the *bardo* of seeking rebirth." In the words of Eliot, from "The Wasteland": "He passed the stages of his age and youth/ entering the whirlpool" (*samsara*).

But Lew's more central teaching, one that was more in line with his *perceptual* Buddhism, was all about how to become free of the world of words, free from one's own subjectivity; in other words, how to reach objective consciousness. In "Everybody Calls Me Tricky, But My Real Name's Mr. Earl: A Sermon", he says:

> Those who live in the words of words kill us who seek
> Union with
> What goes on whether we look at it or not

The teaching given in these lines has two parts to it: That there really is a real world that goes on whether we look at it or not, that it's not all just "in your head"; and that it's important to become consciously one with that world, not just believe in it. The "world of words" is a nice place to visit, though you wouldn't want to live there; yet words were Lew Welch's stock in trade. Given that, as Lew says of "the true rebel" in the same poem, *"And yet he must speak!"*, how can we deal with words so that they will help unite us with, not separate us from, what goes on whether we look at it or not? (And there's still more to "union with what goes on whether we look at it or not." Think about it; it's subtle. If Lew is neither talking about uniting with something by being *aware* of it—nor about the sort of union with a thing we don't have to *seek* because it's already here, since we and it are part of the same world—then what *is* he talking about? How can we unite with something neither physically nor mentally, neither by joining with it nor by becoming aware of it? There's a *koan* for you.)

In order to answer the question "how can words unite us with, not separate us from, what goes on whether we look at it or not?", I need to take a short philosophical detour. (As Lew once said to me, "You have an almost pathological belief in the reality of ideas." I would answer him, now, by saying: "True! There were times when those moths almost ate me to the bone. But you had an almost pathological disbelief in the reality of them because you followed William Carlos Williams' idea of 'no ideas but in things', as if Aristotle could father poets, but not Plato. Why don't you ask Yeats how true that is, if you ever get a chance to meet him?")

The Scholastic Realists (mostly following Plato) said that categories of things are real, which is why we can discern them; all individuals in a given category share a common essence, and that essence is realer than the individuals who make it up. The Scholastic Nominalists (like William of Occam) said that categories of things are conventional, not real; they are arbitrarily conjured up by words alone; the individuals within them share no real common essence.

Realism is intrinsic to the metaphysical worldview, which is inseparable from the notion that levels of being are real, and that higher levels of being are realer than lower ones. It is also the basis of the idea that individuals have *souls*, a "soul" being defined as "a higher level of being resident within a lower one, and expressing itself by means of the lower one." Consequently, most religious worldviews are basically realist.

Nominalism is one of the origins of postmodern nihilism. If only individuals exist, if essences such as "humanity" are unreal, if they are mere names, then to consider a human individual to be in any sense a *person* is unwarranted. And if only individuals are real, then a human being's body must be realer than his soul, his cells realer than his body, the molecules that make up his cells realer than those cells, etc.; corporeal, psychological or spiritual integrity—*unity* of any kind—is an illusion. It's obvious that no essentially religious or spiritual view of things can exist within a Nominalist mindset.

But Realism also has a negative side, spiritually speaking: the *idolatry of abstraction*, the negation of particular individuals in the name of the category they occupy, the false idea that categories, considered to be realer than individuals, are at the same time abstractions drawn *from* individuals rather than higher and more comprehensive levels of individuality itself—concrete living beings who contain, in synthetic mode, all the qualities of all the individuals who share their essence. (William Blake, in his figure of Urizen, god of tyrannical abstraction, and his doctrine of "minute particulars", attacks this kind of idolatry.) In other words, to say—in the name of Realism—that abstraction is realer than individuality, is actually to take a step toward Nominalism. To "abstract" is to discern a common quality in a set of particulars; and if abstract categories are drawn from particulars, not the other way around, then—as the Nominalists claim—those particulars must be realer than their category.

Nominalism, however, also has a spiritually positive side: the potential of demonstrating that the world is real beyond our definitions of it, that if we can free ourselves from the abstract categories in terms of which we experience things—categories that are based mostly on language, and unconscious language at that—then we will see things as they really are.

The Buddhists say: "To name a thing is to kill it," to imprison it inside a lifeless abstraction. Some schools of Hindu thought, in line with the worldviews of most archaic or religiously-based societies, say: "The name of a thing is an intrinsic part of it." According to this theory, to name something is to make it actually present: to name beings is to *summon* them, to *call* them by their names. To ask "What, or by what name, are you called?" is to ask "By what word are you summoned? By what name are you made present?" So the Buddhists, who teach that "all things are without self-nature", have certain affinities with the Nominalists—except that they believe that not only categories but individuals too are unreal (in a sense)—while those who believe that the names of things are real parts of those things are closer to the Realists: only real things can have real names. If the names of things were not intrinsic aspects of them, it would not be possible to assert, as many spiritual traditions do, that "God and His Name are One"; consequently the *dhikr* of the Sufis, the *mnimi Theou* of the Eastern Orthodox Christians, and the *japa-yoga* of the Hindus would be invalid. Nor, in terms of Catholic doctrine, would the Transubstantiation by an ordained priest of simple unleavened wheat bread into the Body of Christ be possible by virtue of the words *Hoc est enim Corpus Meum*. On the other hand, the traditions that assert the "realism of names" also teach that God is absolutely beyond name and form, as in the Hindu practice designated by the words *neti, neti*—"not this, not that"—as well as in such writings as the *Mystical Theology* of Dionysius the Areopagite, that reads just like a Mahayana *sutra*. But if the Buddhists did not also hold in some fashion to the doctrine that "a thing and its name are one," the use of *mantras* would not form so important a part of Mahayana and Vajrayana practice, since *mantras* summon the effective reality of the insight or energy or state of consciousness they designate.

That's the theory, but what about the practice? What is the practical use of the doctrine that "to name something is to kill it," and of the seemingly opposite doctrine that "the name of a thing is an intrinsic part of it"?

The practical use of both doctrines is to free us from the world of words. If we realize that our experience of the world is obscured and conditioned by the verbal definitions we impose upon it, and that those definitions are largely carried by obsessive, unconscious, sub-vocal speech, then we will also realize that to become silent within is to see all things as they really are. So our way is clear.

On the other hand, to understand how the name of something is an intrinsic part of it is to *objectify language*, to get words out of our heads and into the world around us. It is to free language from the grasp of the ego—the little, unconscious, self-identified self that thinks it can call a thing anything it wants to because it *owns language*, because it, not God, is the Creator of the Universe. And once language is released from the grip of the ego, the ego dissolves, because it is (or was) mostly the product of language—of the human identification with, and internalization of, the world around it, by means of language fallen from the level of conscious *summoning* to that of habitual unconscious chatter. If we could name things so consciously and so deliberately that we could actually command their presence—if we could remain in perfect silence until a word of power is born in us, bursting out of us to unite with its object like an arrow to the bull's-eye—then unconscious sub-vocal chatter would be destroyed: this, precisely, is the *tantric* use of human speech. And in order to speak in this way, we will need to understand exactly how, in Lew's words, "To become enamored of our powers is to lose them, at once!", and solve the dilemma he expressed as "How can I learn to get out of my way?" When our naming becomes that power-ful, when it rises from so deep a silence that it can actually com-mand the presence of the thing named, then *we* are no longer speaking; no one is speaking, in such a state, but God Himself.

So perfect silence and perfectly conscious speech ultimately come down to the same thing, spiritually speaking. In meditation we learn that we cannot silence our internal dialogue without listening to it, and that we cannot listen to it unless we are silent. Only in the act of listening can the separation between speech and silence be overcome. Listening, because it annihilates us as speakers, makes words objective to us; they are no longer unconsciously jabbering on inside our heads. Even if we hear them with our inner ear, they are still part of the world around us, like the sound of the traffic or the songs of birds. And if our own internal speech is now outside of us, we are no longer identified with the verbal mind; we are now sitting behind that mind, silently listening to it. And as we listen to it, we simultaneously understand that it is not outside us at all, any more than it is inside us, because there really is no *us*. Our apparently separate identity was composed mostly of words, words we identified with and named with our name—and to *witness* what we once *identified with* is to break that identification and dissolve its (apparent) object. The verbal mind is all we used to be; now that we no longer *are* it, we no longer *are*. And, paradoxically, if we no longer are, then—because self-identification is chaos and the end of self-identification, presence—there we are. This is the Buddhist teaching of *shunyata* and *tathata*, the Sufi teaching of *fana'* (annihilation) and *baqa'* (subsistence in God).

This kind of freedom from the verbal mind and the world it invents is what the Zen *koans* are designed to produce. Two of the three "riddles" Lew composed—"The Riddle of Bowing" and "The Riddle of Hands"—are also designed to set us free from the world of words. Lew said of them: "They are Koans for beginners, making no claim for Perfect Enlightenment, but those who solve them will discover a deep spiritual insight." Here they are:

The Riddle of Bowing

In every culture, in every place and time, there has always been a religion, and in every one of these religions there has always been the gesture of bowing so fully that the forehead strikes the ground.

Why is this?

(There is only one right answer to this riddle)

The Riddle of Hands

In every culture, in every place and time, there has always
been a religion, and in every one of these religions there has
always been the gesture of hands clasped together, as Christians
do to pray.

Why is this?

(There is only one right answer to this riddle)

I must now declare that I am empowered to say "pass" or "fail" to
anyone who wants to tackle these riddles, because Lew told me the
answer to "Bowing" and I solved "Hands" by myself; my solution
was later confirmed by Magda Cregg. All I can say by way of a clue is
that the answers to these riddles are entirely concrete, completely
beyond the world of words, though not (like the true Zen *koans*)
totally beyond the world of form. Each one has only one right
answer. I can't reveal the answers to these riddles because I was
entrusted with them, but I can give you the answer to another riddle, the one that appears in *Wobbly Rock*:

> *Dychymig Dychymig:* (riddle me a riddle)
>
> > Waves and the sea. If you
> > take away the sea
>
> Tell me what it is

The answer is: If you take away "the sea" from "Waves and the
sea," you get "Waves and," which, to the ear, is also "wave-sand". So
the solution is something anyone who has seen a sandy ocean beach
has seen: the pattern of waves, or ripples, left by the ebbing tide in
the drying sand.

This stationary wave-pattern is *tathata*, "suchness"; the absent sea
is *shunyata*, "voidness". *Shunyata* is analogous to the Aristotelian
concept of *being*: that by virtue of which a thing simply is, without
regard to its name or form. *Tathata* is analogous to the Aristotelian
essence: That by virtue of which a thing is what it is, is this but not
that, whether or not it actually exists. To separate *shunyata* from
tathata, Being from Essence—to separate the sea from the waves—
and then reunite them on a higher level, is what all true art does, to

break us free from our habitual ways of looking at things and "cleanse the doors of perception". If we believe that things are heavy literal lumps then we can safely ignore them (we say to ourselves). But if we understand them as *apparitions*, if we see them precisely as "things seen", then we have nowhere to hide from them, and they, no way to hide from us. The Chinese landscape painter, say of the Sung period, renders his pine branches, waterfalls and misty crags simply by removing the *literal Being* of his subject, and leaving only the Essence, the "suchness" of it (though not, of course, the Being of the painting; the Essence of his subject, first given Being by water, timber, rock and air, is now made to Be by ink and rice paper). And when the Essence or *suchness* of, say, a landscape is separated from its *Being*, in the literal sense of that word—separated, in other words, from the unconscious conviction that "of course the landscape *exists*, that goes without saying; so what else is new?"—then the suchness of it can appear purely as *void,* and that voidness be revealed as its true *Being.* The great classical Chinese or Japanese painter does not try to *reproduce* nature, like the "realistic" or "naturalistic" artist, but rather makes a painting which, because it is obviously an "apparition," an image, and not an imitation or counterfeit of a real thing, thereby reveals the essence of its subject—so that, when we find ourselves walking through a landscape of pine trees and waterfalls and misty crags, and suddenly recall such an image, it immediately superimposes itself upon and blends with the picture painted by our senses, since there is no "rivalry of two beings" to prevent it. And so we suddenly witness a world in which Essence fully reveals Being, a world where, in Lew's words, "things *are* exactly what they *seem.*"

This riddle has the virtue, unlike "The Riddle of Hands" and "The Riddle of Bowing", of also being a pun: "waves and/waves sand". Puns were very important to Lew Welch; I could never understand why until now. His puns were not particularly funny, nor were they meant to be—like the last line of "Hiking Poem/High Sierra", "you bear with me". To "bear with" someone is to put up with them, but Lew is also saying that the reader bears the same burden that he does, the burden of being human, a job that sometimes gets to be a real *bear* (not to mention the fact that, in the high Sierras, one might well encounter a bear for real). And once, when

116

as a high school student I showed him an early poem with the word
"groove" in it (in the colloquial Beat/hippy usage), he responded by
saying, "Don't you really mean *grove*?" That wasn't even a pun, it
was only a near-pun. There wasn't anything witty about it, unless he
was covertly pegging me as a Platonist, an "academic" (*academy*, the
name of Plato's school, being from the Greek word for *grove*). But
what was he up to? At least his puns in "[I saw myself]" and "Wobbly Rock" had some real poetic power behind them:

> I saw myself
> a ring of bone
> In the clear stream
> of all of it...
>
> And then heard
> "ring of bone" where
> ring is what a
> bell does

And:

>   Rock
> Returning to the sea, easily, as
> Sea once rose from it. It
> Is a sea rock
>
>   (easily)
>
> I am
> Rocked by the sea

    If to sit on a seat is to be "seated", to sit on a rock is to be "rocked".
To be "rocked by the sea" is to be seated, next to the sea and surrounded by it, on a rock that rocks. And since "by" here means both
"next to" and "through the agency of", Lew might just as well have
said, in the manner of Gertrude Stein, "I am rocked by the sea by
the sea". (See?) But really, why bother incorporating such bathetic
puns into poems that seem to be doing quite well without them? It's
kind of ingenious; it's sort of cute; it's even rather striking in a way
that's hard to describe or account for—but what, if anything, is it
good for?

    What it's good for is to free the reader from the world of words.

Usually, habitually, unconsciously, we identify things with their names. What is a rock? Why it's a *rock*, of course. That heavy solid object sitting there on the seashore is a *rock* and nothing else. What else could it be? But when the same word is presented to us as meaning two or more things at the same time—ring as a round hollow object and ring as a sound, bear as "to carry" and bear as an animal's name, rock as a natural object made of stone and rock as a back-and-forth motion—then the word is separated from its object. And when a word is separated from its object, it becomes an object in itself; it is now *objective* to the listening mind. (Once a word is separated from its object, then—if we so choose—it can be reunited with that object in order to reveal new things about it; a "rock" as a seemingly solid object can now also be seen as something that "rocks" or vibrates back and forth, which is the actual quality of matter as revealed by modern physics, like the pattern of waves left in the sand—but that's not the level of meaning we are considering here and now.)

Lew worked hard at making language *opaque*—something he learned from Gertrude Stein. He said, in *How I Work as a Poet*: "Most people who call themselves poets don't realize that you can't make a poem out of anything except language—any more than a bricklayer can build a brick wall out of anything but bricks". But his language could also be transparent at the same time. The language of, say, Dylan Thomas in his poem "Altarwise by Owl-light"— "Altarwise by owl-light in the half-way house / The gentleman lay graveward with his furies" etc., etc.—is opaque, first because we can't figure out what it means (until later), but more particularly because the images it produces in our minds (its *phanopoeia*) are largely eaten up by its interesting musical language (its *melopoeia*). At the other extreme, the language of some Japanese *haiku* will tend to be completely transparent, its *phanopoeia* dominating and absorbing its *melopoeia*—like this one by Bashō:

> A wild sea—
> In the distance
> Over Sado
> The Milky Way

But at its best, Lew's linguistic opacity is at one with his linguistic transparency, as in this passage from "Wobbly Rock":

Below us:
>   fronds of kelp
>   fish
>   crustaceans
>   eels

Then us
>   then rocks at the cliff's base
>   starfish
>   (hundreds of them sunning themselves)
>   final starfish on the highest rock then

Cliff
>   4 feet up the cliff a flower
>   grass
>   further up more grass
>   grass over the cliff's edge
>   branch of pine then
Far up the sky

>   a hawk

The effect of this union of opacity and transparency is to make his language both concrete, like a plank or a brick, and also empty, like a doorway—a doorway through which we can see the world with various objects in it, among which are the very words Lew is using to describe it. This, along with the riddle and the pun, is another method Lew uses poetry to objectify language, and by so doing free us from the world of words. As he said to me once, "Only poets know that words don't mean anything." He could have meant this in the nihilistic, Nominalist sense that denies the reality of essences or qualities, viewing them as mere verbal abstractions. More likely, however, he meant it in the more-or-less Zen sense: that words are not to be identified with the things they describe, but are to be seen as objects in their own right, like trees or rocks or birds. And if words are also objects, then it is also possible to see, in the Realist sense, that they are the resonant aspects of the very objects they sig-nify—that if a hoot-owl says "Hu" to our outer ears, there is also a way in which, to our inner ear, that a rock is saying "Rock". *We* don't name things; things name themselves *to* us. That's another way of understanding, in poetic mode, how "words don't mean anything."

Furthermore, Lew's teaching designed to free us from the world of words did not always use words exclusively. For example, the first time I met him, in a landscaped garden area at the College of Marin (I was there sitting in for my friend Bill Trumbly, who was too hung over to attend Lew's class; the only other student present was then Dominican nun, and both then and now poet, Mary Norbert Körte), he said: "Take a look at those trees over there. Now imagine the spaces between the trees as solid objects, and the trees them-selves as empty spaces." And we did it; we saw as he saw. In so doing, we perceptually actualized (I realized later) the famous line "form is emptiness, emptiness is form" from the *Heart Sutra*, and learned how to see the world not as a set of literal objects—as our uncon-scious identification of things with our names for them had taught us to do—but rather as an *apparition*, as *Maya*. Like Lew said, "I try to write from the poise of mind that lets me see how things are exactly what they seem"—not how they *are* what they *are*, but how they *are* what they *seem*—in view of the fact that what they *are* is, precisely, a *seeming*. That perceptual seed Lew planted in my psyche—a little like those shamanic perception exercises designed to deconstruct the world in Carlos Castaneda's *Journey to Ixtlan* (though Lew taught me his own exercise way before Castaneda's first book *The Teachings of Don Juan* came out)—sprouted years later, when, meditating with my eyes open in a redwood grove in Gerstle Park in San Rafael, California, the redwood grove was sud-denly transformed into a birch grove: the redwood trees, empty; the spaces between them, birch trees.

A deeper and more complete perception exercise—or at least the suggestion for one—appears in "Wobbly Rock":

> On a trail not far from here
> Walking in meditation
> We entered a dark grove
> And I lost all separation in step with the
> Eucalyptus as the trail walked back beneath me...

What exactly is happening here? The perceiver's sense of himself as an object walking through a eucalyptus grove is replaced by the sense that the perceiver is motionless—except for his legs' stride—and that the eucalyptus grove and the ground it rises from are moving backwards, beneath him and past him. This experience is analogous to that of the Mevlevi or "whirling" dervishes when they practice their "turning" exercise. To begin with it seems to the dervish as if the environment were stationary and he turning counterclockwise—but then a perceptual shift occurs: now the dervish is standing still, and the world is turning around him, clockwise; he has become "the still point of the turning world." (Interestingly, if the dervish stops turning before this shift occurs he will become dizzy, but if stops after the shift, no dizziness is experienced.) The Buddhist take on such perceptual shifts, the dialectic of it, goes something like this: "We habitually base our sense of reality on our perception of things. But if this perception can be completely altered (by intoxicants, by yogic practices, or simply by turning our head to look in another direction), then it disappears as an absolute criterion for what is real. Consequently there is no way we can say for sure either that the perceiver is moving and the world is stationary, or that the world is moving and the perceiver is stationary. All we have are patterns of perception. These patterns cannot be called 'objective', since they can be altered at will by the subject, but neither can they be called 'subjective', since they include both subject and object, both perceiver and world, and the world is something that 'goes on whether we look at it or not.' Conclusion: the world and the one perceiving it are not *literally* real; they are empty apparitions arising in the One Mind." Lew's own rendition of this dialectic appears in his poem "Four Studies in Perception"; the setting is Golden Gate Park, San Francisco:

> A grove of Laurel grows in the city park.
> It grows whether I look at it or not,
> By a path deliberately unintended (unattended).
>
> I can find it.   I can see it.   I can sing:
>
> *Magical Tree!*
> *Leaf in my mother's stew!*

Crown!   Chew
Thy leaves to brighten
color in my eyes?

But all of it,
Singer, Song, the Grove itself
disappears, instantly,
if only I look another way.

If I only look another way, I make
Bulldozers, Baseball Players, and, later
Owls

There is also a Hindu explanation for the perceptual shift experienced by the whirling dervish or the meditative walker: "When the *Atman* dawns—the Unseen Seer, the Absolute Witness who is the One Self of All—it is He who is motionless, and the Universe who moves. He is impassive, adamantine *Shiva*: She is powerful, dancing *Shakti*. He is the Rock, but She does all the Rocking".

Lew Welch's worldview, and his teaching, were based on three things: A personal myth that died with him (first "Leo" and then "Turkey Buzzard"); a more-or-less Neo-Pagan earth-worship that had some value for opening our eyes to the world around us, but that finally made it intolerable for Lew to live in a time of environmental degradation, since if there is no God Who is beyond this world as well as within it, if this world is all there is, then the decay of the earth is, effectively, the decay of Reality itself; and his own unique brand of perceptual Buddhism, which was a real contribution to the way of Perfect Total Enlightenment. May what was mortal in his teaching die forever; may what was immortal in his teaching enlighten us, and him.

Addendum: From Correspondence

Lew Welch, in *I Remain* (his collected correspondence, which I never read) apparently named me his "successor", which would make me the "one with proper instructions for [his] continuance" mentioned in "Song of the Turkey Buzzard".

So what's this "continuance" thing? Is it just memory, the well-known "poetic immortality" whereby the august ghosts of the *pitri-yana*, the Giant Dead, are held in shape by the praise of the living, suspended between two worlds? Or is there something more to it, something that has to do with final Liberation?

I remember a vision I had of Lew on one occasion when I threw into the fire burning on my hearth a Turkey Buzzard feather he had "given" me during a hike in the California woods; I heard him say: "Things don't change here as fast as I thought they would." So *continuance* is apparently needed—letting go and moving on.

My main interest in writing about Lew has been to show the metaphysical/philosophical side, or core, of him, who was by far the most metaphysical of the Beats (except perhaps Kerouac, whom everybody nowadays just identifies with the "wow" of experience), though he deliberately hid it—as he also hid his exquisite poetic ear—in a seemingly prosaic if not rather dumb and simple-minded style. (Ferlinghetti said that to me once: "Welch? He's just dumb.") Lew wanted to TRANSMIT truth, not just get us to think about it. Nowadays, however, poetry is not supposed to transmit concepts, especially sophisticated ones—"didactic" is a pejorative term—so no more Dante, no more Shakespeare, no more Blake. Our controllers, the dumbers-down of America (and the world) have spoken, and we obey. Of course Lew, like the Zen people, also wanted to transmit truth beyond concepts . . . but if we are never allowed to get to real ideas, how can we ever get beyond them?

People who commit suicide like Lew did tend to get stuck in a feedback loop of "intending not to exist", which doesn't work very well because in order to intend not to exist you have to exist so you can intend that etc., etc., etc.—part of the same dilemma that Lew expressed, in "Leo's Poet-Plight", as:

> . . . the question only a German could ask:
> *How can you try not to try?*

By "continuance" Lew might have meant "continuance in human memory", but the inner meaning is "continuance on the Path", the path of self-uninvention, which he rather injudiciously eschewed in "The Entire Sermon by the Red Monk", because he'd gotten to Leo

123

and liked it there. What, did he think Leo was going to last forever? Where's your Buddhism, Lew? Turkey Buzzard was a definite step, but there's a lot more steps after that.

I believe that Lew "ate" a big chunk of my karma, the karma of the *puer aeternus*, the lyric poet who dies young, like Keats did, "half in love with easeful death". He did it so I didn't have to, and I am now duty-bound to return the favor by helping him move.

~~ 11 ~~

The Dark Side of Poetry: Terence McKenna, DMT, the Techno-Elves, and the Deconstruction of the Human Form

THE following text is excerpted from a talk on the effects of the psychedelic DMT (dimethyltryptamine) given by ethnobotanist, "psychonaut" and rumored CIA mouthpiece Terrence McKenna, who died in the year 2000. It was transcribed from a fractal animation composition by Martin Stebbing that I viewed on You Tube at: https://www.youtube.com/watch?v=8veXhlhXBjQ; Dr. McKenna's lecture formed part of the sound track. DMT is the "natural psychedelic" present in the human brain; it plays a role in the process of dreaming:

> You might think if you've never had a psychedelic experience that . . . you rise into the realms of light and union with the Deity or something like that . . . that's not what happens on DMT; what happens on DMT [is that] a troop of elves smashes down your front door and rotates and balances the wheels on the after-death vehicle, present[s] you with the bill and then depart[s]. . . .
>
> It doesn't seem to affect your mind . . . you don't change under the influence of DMT . . . you don't change, [rather] the world is completely replaced . . . and not one iota of what is put in its place is taken from this world . . . language has evolved in this world and it can serve no other . . . what you are looking at is literally the unspeakable. . . .
>
> There are entities there . . . they are in your face . . . worse than in your face, because what they do is they jump into your chest,

125

and then they jump out . . . the entities speak to you . . . both in English and in another way, but in English what they say is . . . "pay attention, pay attention" . . . they are trying to show you something . . . they say "don't just spiral off into amazement and start raving about God and all that, *forget* that" . . . they are bounding toward you, jumping into your chest, bounding away, and they offer, they make offerings, and they love you . . . they say this, they say "we love you, you come so rarely . . . welcome, welcome" . . . and then they make these offerings, and the offerings are objects of some sort . . . remember, you are not changed, you are exactly the person you were a few minutes before . . . and the objects they offer are like Fabergé eggs, or exquisitely tooled and enameled pieces of machinery . . . these objects are themselves somehow alive, and transforming, changing . . . and you have this realization, if I could get this thing back to my world history would never be the same, a single one of these objects . . . would confound my world beyond hope of recovery . . . the creatures . . . are singing, they are speaking in a kind of translinguistic glossalalia, they are actually making these objects with their voices . . . they are singing these things into existence and what the message is, is "do what we are doing, you can do what we are doing, DO IT!" . . . [then] something comes out of you . . . and you discover you can do it, that you can use language to condense objects into this space, it's the dream of all magic . . . they go mad with delight . . . they all jump into your chest at once . . . what these creatures want, according to them, is that they want us to transform our language somehow . . . clearly we need to transform our language because our culture is created by our language, and our culture is toxic, murderous and on a downhill bummer . . . how does this relate to the persistent idea promulgated by Robert Graves and other people that there is a primal language of poetry, that poetry as we know it is a pale pale thing, and that at some time in the human past people were in command of languages which literally compelled belief . . . because they don't make an appeal through argument or metaphor, they compel belief because they are able to present themselves as imagery. . . .

[But] why is there this urgency on the part of these entitles, and who exactly and what exactly are they. . . .?

What they are is, precisely, the Jinn. The Jinn are conscious entities inhabiting the subtle, or animic, or psychic, or intermediary plane; as Dr. McKenna correctly says, they have nothing to do with the realms of light or union with the Deity. The Jinn are the beings who inspired the pre-Islamic poets of Arabia, in the "time of ignorance" before the Qur'an descended, spoken as it was *in the clear Arabic tongue*, in a time when poetry was tantamount to magic, as it was with the Druids, and still is in the world of the Shamans. This same class of beings, contacted via the ouija board, were responsible for James Merrill's award-winning epic poem, *The Changing Light at Sandover*. Once, while I was reading *Islam, Arabs, and the Intelligent World of the Jinn* by Amira El-Zein, the Jinn came to me in a dream, promising to make me the greatest poet of the age if I would make pact with them, assuring me that I would become universally known as the composer of huge brilliant transhuman epics; they gave me a single line of all that vast unwritten literature as a sample of their wares: "*their great sapphire searchlights/sweeping the Giant Dead....*"

Why are they so happy when we visit them? Because they need us, desperately. They say they love us, and indeed they do; they love us like a hungry wolf loves a cut of raw sirloin. They want to Jinnify us, they want to *turn us into them*; they jump in and out of our chests in order to transmute our human hearts into Jinnish hearts, to make us *changelings*; they offer us their magical linguistic technologies because they want to replace human language with Jinnish language. But why? If they have all those amazing powers, those "wild talents", what do they need with bourgeois, prosaic, boring, slowpoke humanity? Aren't they happy with all their fascinating, kaleidoscopic, sentient Fabergé eggs in their own colorful world? Perhaps they want to supplant human language because, even this late in the cycle, it still shows traces of its Divine origin, especially truly sacred languages like Hebrew, Sanskrit and Arabic—this last being the chosen language for the Holy Qur'an, the theophany of the Spirit of Allah in human language itself. And exactly what is the "bill" they present us with after we have absorbed their entertainment? If they agreed to spin the straw of our dull everyday lives into gold, did we promise them our first-born sons?

They need us because we possess what the Muslims call the *amanah*, the Trust—something that they once held in the aeon previous to this one, but lost through the false belief that they were the creators rather than Allah. And this can be largely confirmed if we take a look into their world through the window of the UFO/alien abduction phenomenon rather than that of the DMT experience. The techno-elves of the DMT dimension offered Terrence McKenna Fabergé eggs made by their own speech and song, after which the same ability to generate such multi-dimensional poetic creations was *drawn out of him*, making him partly elflike in the process. Likewise the "aliens" who abduct people are often seen to draw eggs and sperm out of them, resulting in the creation of imaginal infants which the abductees recognize as alien/human hybrids—in other words, changelings. To hold the Trust means to recognize oneself, in common with all the creatures of the universe, as a word spoken by God, and furthermore to see oneself as the synthesis of all of God's creative words in a single Human Form, and thus as His *khalifa* or viceregent in the manifest, dimensional cosmos. *Lo! We offered the trust unto the heavens and the earth and the hills, but they shrank from bearing it and were afraid of it. And man assumed it. Lo! he hath proved a tyrant and a fool.* (Q.33:72) If, however, we forget that we are words spoken by God, and see ourselves instead as the First Speakers—which is, precisely, the temptation of magic—then we will lose the Trust, and so become, like the Jinn who held the *amanah* in a former age, mere ghosts—or rather *elves*—of our former selves. As we begin to lose the human form to the "transhuman" reality of our own creations, as we see the words we speak appearing as real, almost sentient objects in the space of technology, and history, and ultimately the human body itself—via computers, for example—then we come near to forfeiting the Trust. And the Jinn apparently believe (quite foolishly so, however) that if we lose it will return to them again, making their race the new and restored *khalifa* of God's creation. That's why they feel the urgent need to draw us into their world: so they can tempt us to jettison the Human Form. But how can they legitimately act as *khalifa* of Allah again when they were willing to tell McKenna: "Don't just spiral off into amazement and start raving about God and all that, *forget* that"? Seeing themselves, not God, as the creators was what lost them the *amanah* in the first place—and now they expect to regain the Trust simply because they see the human race as about to make the same mistake they did? They think that if they can cause us to forget God, partly by convincing us that they themselves, not God, are our creators (a common motif in UFO/alien mythology), thereby causing us to lose our grip on the Trust, they will somehow be able to pick it up after we drop it. And they want to steal back the Trust from the human race with great urgency because they feel our common psycho-physical world coming to an end. Perhaps some of them believe that this world, or a residue of it, can be saved if only the human race can be transformed into the Jinn; the space aliens often make the same claim for their human/alien hybridization project. Others, however, undoubtedly know the truth: that the end of this cycle of manifestation will inevitably reveal Allah, not them, as *Maliki yawm al-Din*, Owner of the Day of Judgment, and *Rabb al-Alamin*, Lord of the Worlds. So their attempt to Jinnify us, to turn us into changelings, is really rather foolish. If they were to succeed in spreading their betrayal of the Trust laid on them by God in a former age throughout the entire cosmos, tearing the *amanah* from the grasp of every sentient and God-fearing race in the universe, not even that would win them even the first foothold on their hopeless ascent back to the Deity they rejected, much less give them the power to replace Him! Allah speaks out of Silence and *by* Silence—and Silence is one skill that the Jinn have never mastered.

McKenna speaks of an age when speech compelled belief: not because what it told was *true*—considerations such as "truth" pertain only to the realms of light, and are consequently irrelevant to the agenda of the techno-elves—but because it spoke in a language of images, and images are taken by the mind, largely by the right brain, as the literal flora and fauna of mental reality; there is no way you can *refute* an image. It is this aspect of imagery which has beguiled, and enlisted the skills and energies, of many of today's propagandists, social engineers and technological mind-controllers, who most certainly want to gain, or re-gain, the power to *compel belief*.

The great temptation of our time, the time of the *fitan* or Tribulation before the arrival of the Hour, is to seek the illusion of freedom (or perhaps only the illusion of *safety*) by abandoning the Human Form. The last surah of the Qur'an, *Mankind*, was sent precisely to protect us from this temptation:

> *Say: I seek refuge in the Lord of mankind*
> *The King of mankind,*
> *The God of mankind,*
> *From the evil of the sneaking whisperer,*
> *Who whispers in the hearts of mankind,*
> *Of the Jinn and of mankind.*

> —Surah al-Naas

❧ 12 ❧

Sufism, Spiritual Romance, and the Union of East and West

Partly excerpted from *Shadow of the Rose: The Esoterism of the Romantic Tradition*, Sophia Perennis, 2008, and *Vectors of the Counter-Initiation: The Course and Destiny of Inverted Spirituality*, Sophia Perennis, 2012

ONE clear cultural chain linking Europe and the Muslim world, partly through the great international marketplace of al-Andalus, is the *silsilah* of Spiritual Romance. And among the most skillful and dedicated smiths of this chain were the Sufis, and their secret brothers in the West who went by other names, or by no name at all.

Arabo-Persian music and poetry exerted a great influence upon European art, culture and spirituality, and became one of the central tributaries to the western Romantic tradition. In its essence—speaking in alchemical terms—western Romance was the marriage of the ancient lore of the Celts (*Quicksilver*, the Bride) with militant and chivalrous Islam (*Sulfur*, the Groom) within the *athenor* of medieval Christendom: and the witnessing Priest of that union was Jesus Christ, who called his followers the *Salt* of the earth. By "Romantic" I am of course referring, in literary terms, not to the English and German poets of the Romantic Era, but to the original medieval *romances* dedicated to chivalric love and the Grail quest, by such authors as Robert de Boron, Chrétien de Troyes, Sir Thomas Mallory and Wolfram von Eschenbach, in which human love was often taken both as a symbol and as a concrete expression and instance of Divine Love and the Spiritual Path. Western Romance began with the troubadours, and came to its highest station of development in the *Vita Nuova* and the *Divina Commedia* of Dante

131

Alighieri, the only western poet who deserves to share with Jalalluddin Rumi the title of "greatest spiritual poet of all time."

The troubadour convention of the beloved but unattainable Lady was foreshadowed by the *udhri* poets of 11th-century Islam, who deferred to and idealized their chosen Ladies in terms nearly identical to those used by the western troubadours, and considered romantic love as one of the most powerful ways of developing and refining the human character. (The Lady cannot be attained on the lover's own initiative, but must *grant* her favors, and remains entirely free to grant or to withhold them; she is legitimately comparable to God in this respect.) According to Idries Shah (who got *some* things right), the very concept of the western "love-song" may ultimately be of Sufi origin.

The Arabo-Persian-Sufic literary and musical influence, essential to the development of the troubadour tradition, influenced the chivalric romances as well. It entered Europe through several doors: through the crusades, through the culturally Islamicized imperial court of Frederick II in the Kingdom of Sicily (which included much of the Italian peninsula), and through Muslim Spain. A system of sentiments with affinities to that of the *udhri* poets was expressed by the Andalusian writer Ibn Hazm in his book *The Dove's Neck-ring*, which is thought to be the direct ancestor of *The Art of Loving Honestly* by Andreas Capellanus, the central prose textbook of western Courtly Love, commissioned by Eleanor of Aquitaine herself. Nor was the western romantic tradition without its "initiatory" chains-of-transmission, comparable in many ways to those of *Tasawwuf* and possibly developed in imitation of them. Capellanus, Dante, Boccaccio, Guido Cavalcanti, the painter Pedro de Pisa, Petrarch, Cardinal Francesco Barberino, Dino Compagni and Brunetto Latini are thought by some scholars to have been members of a spiritual brotherhood known as the Fedeli d'Amore or Fede Santa, a semi-secret initiatory order which used both the allegory and the actual practice of romantic love as a spiritual method. The Provençal troubadour Arnaut Daniel (*floruit* c. 1180–1200) may have transmitted, via the Fedeli d'Amore of which he was likely a member, spiritual love-lore influenced by the Sufis to his successor Fedele, Dante Aligheri, who extols him as the greatest of the troubadours (*il miglior fabbro*, "the greater craftsman") in his *Purgatorio*. Such great figures in Sufism as Ruzbehan Baqli have been classed by some (Henry Corbin, for example) as among "the Fedeli d'Amore of Islam," while affinities and possible ties have been discerned by certain scholars between the western Fedeli d'Amore and the Knights Templars, the flower of western chivalry, who are reputed to have made esoteric spiritual contact with Islam even while fighting against it in the Crusades. The Fedeli d'Amore are sometimes even characterized as a Third (lay) Order of the Templars. In the words of one "initiate" who wishes to remain anonymous,

> It is said that the three secrets of the Fedeli d'Amore were: Love, Beauty and the Heart. Suhrawardi [*the Persian Sufi and* Ishraqi *or* "*Illuminist*"] speaks of Beauty, Love and Nostalgia [*which perhaps refers to "remembrance" in its spiritual sense—the Sufi* dhikr, *the Hesychast* mnimi Theou]. This is the visible, communicable secret. The second secret, reserved for the initiates, is that one must learn how to read the rule of divine Love in the book of human love. The third secret belongs to adepts. It is the Faith of the Faithful, which is the direct vision of God in a human form, beautiful to contemplate, but without the agitation of the carnal nature [*precisely as Dante contemplated his Beatrice, and Ibn al-'Arabi his Nizam*].... The Fedeli d'Amore appeared to the later Sufis as an unexpected variant of the Shadhiliyya; their particular way of symbolically mixing love and poetry is common to both systems.

One of the most direct encounters between the Arabo-Persian poets and singers and the western troubadours, and thus the world of western Romance, came about in the following way. The father of Guillem de Poitiers, Duke of Aquitaine (d. 1126), "the first troubadour"—who was the grandfather of Eleanor of Aquitaine—won from a Spanish emir in one of the many feudal skirmishes of the time a troupe of singing-girls, who would have known, between them, hundreds of songs at the very least. Guillem grew up in a palace surrounded by these women; in effect, they were his nannies. This is the most direct link we know of between the poetry of the troubadours and the Arabo-Persian tradition, filled with Sufi lore, that it so closely resembles. Guillem was also a student of Neo-

Platonism, a tradition that greatly influenced Sufic modes of expression, though the doctrine and practice of *Tasawwuf* remained for the most part firmly rooted in Islam. And if the history of my mother's family compiled by my great aunt is accurate, I am 29th in direct (though often female) line from Eleanor of Aquitaine, and thus 31st in line from Guillem de Poitiers, the first troubadour.

In any case, the influence of Arabo-Persian Sufi poetry upon the western Romantic tradition was deep and widespread. Elizabethan poetry was greatly enriched by it, partly through the poetic tradition of Italy; some of the sonnets of Shakespeare read like Sufi *ghazals* (lyric poems with romantic, nostalgic, or elegiac themes), a form that may in fact have been the ancestor of the Petrarchian sonnet, the model on which the Elizabethan sonnet form is based. And as late as the 20th century, Sufi themes, though probably not recognized as such, still appeared in the Spanish poetry of Antonio Machado and Juan Ramón Jiménez, as witness this lyric by Machado:

> Wayfarer, the only way
> is your footsteps, there is no other.
>
> Wayfarer, there is no way,
> you make the way by walking.
> As you go, you make the way
> and stopping to look behind,
> you see the path that your feet
> will never travel again.
>
> Wayfarer, there is no way—
> Only foam trails in the sea.

This poem, though it does not recognize the formal existence of a *tariqa* with its way stations and *maqamat*, perfectly renders the Sufic sense of "solitude-in-company", the solitude of the human Heart in the presence of Allah. On the Spiritual Path we are capable of taking first one faltering step and then another only by His guidance and command. We can never anticipate these commands and insights, but must accept and obey them exclusively in the *waqt*, the eternal present moment of spiritual time. I hazard to say that the

Spanish quality of *soledad* grew in part out of the solitude of the Sufi, a solitude that led the famous woman Sufi Rabi'a al-Adawiyya of Iraq to write:

> I am a stranger in Your country
> And lonely among Your worshippers:
> This is the substance of my complaint.

Though the ethos of romantic Courtly Love grew up in southern France, its greatest literary expression (outside of the *Divine Comedy*)—namely Wolfram's *Parzival*—was German; ultimately it was better served by Teutonic earnestness than by French exquisitry. But, speaking for myself, I feel nearer the mark when I say, simply, that the spirit of Romance is Spanish. Its direct ancestors were the poets of Muslim Spain, and no short poem better renders the heart of romantic passion, in all its aristocratic unsentimentality, than these lines by Abu-l-Hasan ibn al-Qabturnuh (in Lysander Kemp's translation):

> I remembered Sulayma when the passion
>   of battle was as fierce
> as the passion of my body when we parted.
>
> I thought I saw, among the lances, the tall
>   perfection of her body,
> and when then bent toward me, I embraced them.

In these six lines are contained the root of the whole matter—just as, in Ibn al-'Arabi's phrase, the whole of the coming day is contained in the first light of dawn. And even though this is not necessarily strictly a Sufi poem, the poetry of Muslim Spain was so soaked with spiritual lore (like that of the Elizabethans, notably Donne and Shakespeare) that it can be read esoterically as follows: Sulayma is God, and the ranks of the enemy are this world. As soon as we agreed to be created, on the day when God asked us *Am I not your Lord?* and we all answered *Yea!* (Q. 7:172), we were required to leave the bed of pre-eternal Union, mount the steed of the human body, and ride out into this world of existence and conflict. We will either mistake this profoundly engaging and distracting world for God, and so forget Him, or recognize it as made up of nothing but the signs of His secret Presence, and so begin to remember. If we

135

mistake this world for God, we will die in darkness. If, on the other hand, the curtain of this world is torn to unveil the face of God as She who "looketh forth as the morning, fair as the moon, clear as the sun, *terrible as an army with banners*" (Song of Solomon 6:10), then we will die before we die. This poem can be further understood, on an even more esoteric level, as referring to the alternation between a spiritual state of expansion, produced by an unveiling of God's Beauty, and one of contraction, under the influence of God's Majesty—as well as to the phenomenon, well known to mystics, that a period of spiritual exaltation will often herald a renewed attack from the *nafs al-ammara bi'l su*, "the self commanding to evil", which can drive one to despair unless it too is recognized as a face of Allah: "Who loves me not in My Wrath will never love Me in My Mercy." The ethos of Love and Death is the essence of Romance; it is also the essence of *Tasawwuf*, whose method is *Mahabbah*, Divine Love, and whose ultimate goal is *Fana'*, Annihilation in God.

Before the "discovery" of the greatest Sufi poet, Jalaluddin Rumi—who was also the greatest poet of the Persian language—by Reynold Nicholson, translator of the *Mathnavi*, and Rumi's later popularization (in partly bastardized form) by such American poets as Robert Bly and Coleman Barks, Rumi was known to Goethe (1749–1832), Persian poetry being the main influence upon his collection of poems *West-Oestlichen Divan*; Emerson (1803–1882) and the New England Transcendentalists were familiar with this poetic tradition as well.

Apart from these well-known writers who consciously turned to Sufi works for spiritual sustenance, the unacknowledged influence of Sufi poetry also persisted in the west far into the 20th century through the "literary ballad" tradition and its influence on popular song. A good example is the song "Plaisir d'Amour", written in 1780 by Jean Paul Égide Martini, and recorded, partly in English translation, by Joan Baez:

> The joys of love
> Are but a moment long;
> The pain of love endures
> The whole life long.

Your eyes kissed mine
I saw the love in them shine;
You brought me heaven right there when
Your eyes kissed mine.

My love loves me,
A world of wonder I see;
A rainbow shines through my window;
My love loves me.

And now he's gone,
Like a dream that fades in the dawn;
But the words stay locked in my heartstrings:
My love loves me.

Compare this song to the following quatrains of Rumi:

Remembrance of you only hides you from me, Beloved.
The lightning of your face only veils that face, Beloved.
Remembering your lips, I know I am without them;
To remember your lips is to lose those lips, Beloved.

I am Love's Lover—and Love? He loves me too.
Flesh is lover to soul, and soul to flesh.
Sometimes I circle his neck with my two arms;
Sometimes he pulls on my coat, as lovers will.

By your step the dust of earth became green and happy;
Pregnant with joy, a hundred buds were born.
By your step the stars and the heavens all shouted together;
Inside that clamor, a star caught a glance from the Moon.

Since God has written "soon we will part" on the Tablet,
Why then all this conflict and violence, my friend?
If I've been bad for you, soon you'll escape that annoyance—
And if I've been good, then our love will live in your memory.

Another example is the poem "I Shall Not Care" by Sarah Teasdale (1884–1933), set to music and recorded in 1967 by Tom Rapp of the folk-rock band Pearls Before Swine:

When I am dead
And over me bright April
Shakes out her rain-drenched hair,

Though you should lean
Above me broken-hearted,
I shall not care
(I shall not care.)

....

I shall have peace
As leafy trees are peaceful
When rain bends down the bough;
And I shall be
More silent and cold-hearted
Than you are now
(Than you are now.)

Compare these quatrains of Rumi, where (given that God is better than any of us at playing hard-to-get) the same sentiment is expressed, but not the same conclusion:

Though love and faith bind me to you
—you endlessly tormenting beauty—
Still, I am patient. But aren't you ashamed,
Even for one day, of the pain you've dealt my heart?

"If I keep apart from my beloved", I said to myself
"Maybe he will miss me".
I strove much and endured much, but failed in everything:
How can I ever hide myself from You?

The heart that's ruined by those lips
Will never wander in the garden, in springtime, again.
The branches of the trees prostrate, endlessly, endlessly,
To the power of the wind.

The day you pass by my tomb, sit down and admit
That by making me want you, it was you who killed me.
Then I can shout from the earth with which I am blended:
"O my lost one! My Joseph of the age!"

[These and the Rumi quatrains above are based on the translations of Ibrahim W. Gamard and A.G. Rawan Farhadi, from *The Quatrains of Rumi: Ruba 'iat-e Jalaluddin Muhammad Balkhi-Rumi*, Sufi Dari Press, 2008, as "transcreated" by myself.]

Sufism, Spiritual Romance, and the Union of East and West

Romance in the west always had an uneasy relationship with the Catholic Church, just as Sufism did with exoteric Islam. The Sufis were almost always orthodox Muslims, whose spirituality was the sometimes unrecognized but always legitimate expression of the central truth of the Islamic religion, based in large part on an esoteric hermeneutic of the Noble Qur'an. Romance in the west, however, was less fully Catholic than Sufism was Islamic, at least before Dante ultimately synthesized them. To take one example, it formed an integral part of the culture of southern France which spawned the heretical Cathars or Albigenses; it was only after Provence was forcibly re-Catholicized by the Albigensian Crusade—the only crusade launched against an entirely European enemy—that the troubadours took the Blessed Virgin, not the wife of some local lord, as their Lady. And it is important as well not to identify Sufism with "spiritual romance" exclusively, since philosophical or metaphysical intelligence, as well as rigorous ascetic sobriety, were and are equally integral parts of that tradition.

It may be because of the uncertain relationship in the west of romance—spiritual or humanly erotic—to Christian orthodoxy that we tend to see Rumi and his compatriots as rebels against orthodox Islam; however, this is almost entirely false. Persian poetry, like the Song of Solomon, was capable of employing human eros as a metaphor for the love of God in a way and to a degree that is almost inconceivable to us in our own secular, post-Christian society. It is we who can hardly imagine any more a love that is not immediately reducible to sex, not Jalalluddin Rumi. His love for Shams Tabrizi, his spiritual master, was both unashamedly passionate and almost entirely transpersonal; Rumi mourned his disappearance not because he had lost a love-object, but because he had lost the mirror within which, whenever he chose or was permitted to look, he might see the face of God. If the troubadours had all been monks instead of philandering aesthetes, they would have been much closer in terms of Christianity to what the Sufis were, and are, in terms of Islam.

As we have already seen, Love and Death are the essence of both Romance and the Spiritual Path. The great modern essay of Love and Death is "The Duende: Theory and Divertissement" by Federico García Lorca. In it he speaks of the quality of this passion as the dark, Divine power that inspires all truly Spanish poetry, music and dance, as well as the art of bullfighting; in line with Spanish folklore he names it the *Duende*, which is sometimes thought of as a kind of elf or household spirit. He writes:

> In all Arabian music, in the dances, songs and elegies of Arabia, the coming of the *Duende* is greeted with fervent cries of *Allah! Allah! God! God!*, so close to the *Ole! Ole!* of our bull rings that who is to say that they are not actually the same; and in all the songs of southern Spain the appearance of the *Duende* is followed by heartfelt expressions of *God alive!*—profound, human, tender, the cry of communion with God through the medium of the five senses.... [from the Grove Press edition of *The Poet in New York*, Ben Belitt's translation, pp. 158–159]
>
> The *Duende* will not approach at all if he does not see the possibility of violent death, if he is not convinced he will circle death's house.... [Ibid., p. 162]

Duende, in Spanish, is short for *duen de la casa*, "Lord of the House", which, in Islam, is specifically a title of Allah, as in the Sufi saying attributed to the poetess Rabi'a al-Adawiyya, "first the Lord, then the House". The House is precisely the Kaaba, draped in black, perpetually circled by pilgrims, dressed in their white funeral shrouds. And so Lorca, eight-hundred years of Muslim Spain still in his blood, reveals to us the essence of Romantic passion as a true name of God, whose reverberation, in the human Heart, is *ishk*, passionate love—a word that literally denotes the way a vine will hug and wrap itself around a tree, sometimes killing it. It is God's Beauty opening, like a wound, to reveal His Majesty; it is God's Wrath blossoming, like a rose, to reveal His Mercy, which eternally rules it. If His Mercy has precedence over His Wrath, then His Wrath is the servant of His Mercy—and if, *insha'Allah*, He chooses to reveal this secret to us, then we may yet retain our humanity, and the sacred Trust it bears, through the terror of these times.

✺ 13 ✺

The Spiritual Exercises of Lew Welch: Essays in Perceptual Buddhism

Drawn from *Ring of Bone, Collected Poems* (New & Expanded Edition) by Lew Welch, City Lights Publishers, 2012, and from the Oral Tradition. Some of these exercises also appear in the chapter "Lew Welch as Teacher", where they are presented in the context of language and its effect on perception. Here we are considering them outside that context, as perception exercises pure and simple.

WHEN I was a Catholic high school student in the 1960's in Marin County, California, I was privileged to encounter Beat Generation poet Lew Welch. A friend of mine had phoned me to say that he was too hung-over to attend Lew's poetry class at the College of Marin, so he suggested that I take his place. And so, in a landscaped garden on the College grounds, I met Lew; the only other student present was Dominican nun and poet Mary Norbert Körte. Unexpectedly, this strange... intense... raw-boned... plainly emphatic... deliberately concrete... painstakingly simple man seemed more interested in teaching us perception exercises than in talking about poetry; still, I gave him some copies of my own poems for his perusal.

A short time later Lew rang me up to say, "you can be a poet if you want to", and then took me under his wide, sometimes shaky, and always superlatively alcoholic wing. He mentored me as a poet during the last years of his life, reciting me the classics (Burroughs, Yeats and others) and also passing on many of the spiritual insights he'd come to over the years. But it was only in 2011 that I was told by a correspondent that Lew, in *I Remain*, his collected letters (a book I've never read), had named me his "heir". I can't claim to be his heir as a poet since my style is quite different from his, so I have decided to fulfill the duty he laid upon me by composing the present essay, hoping to highlight the spiritual exercises that appear here and there in his poetry, hidden in plain sight. Lew Welch conceived and transmitted a form of *perceptual Buddhism*, imminently practical and entirely compatible with classical Buddhism, Zen in particular. These exercises, if practiced successfully, will accomplish the central Zen task of ridding the mind (temporarily at least) of abstract philosophical ideas and other forms of mental trash. By "perceptual Buddhism" I mean a way of seeing the world around us that teaches impermanence, *anitya*, and the voidness of phenomena, *shunyata*. Our conceptual minds—our verbal minds, that is—try to fix and solidify things by *naming* them, thus turning them into concepts. A rock becomes a "rock", not the actual complex, ongoing, unending process we name by that name. And because we think we know *what* it is, we forget to remember *that* it is. We file it away under "been there, done that", and don't really see it any more. (This may be why one of Lew's compact, one-line aphorisms was: "Only poets know that words don't mean anything.")

The perception exercises of Lew Welch are designed to cut through that kind of amnesia.

ONE

Step Out onto the Planet

This is a preliminary exercise for people who spend too much time indoors, fiddling with computers or watching TV. Some readers may have encountered it before since it's been posted a number of places on the Web:

Step out onto the planet.
Draw a circle a hundred feet round.

Inside the circle are
Three hundred things nobody understands, and, maybe
Nobody's ever really seen.

How many can you find?

[Don't just read this, do it. Do it in a group. Do it for an hour or more. No talking.]

TWO

TreeSee

The day I first met Lew, and sat with him in that landscaped garden, he said to us: "Take a look at those trees over there. Now imagine the spaces between the trees as solid objects, and the trees themselves as empty spaces." And we did it; we saw as he saw.

That's the practice. It can be done in a group, or alone. It's basically an expression—concrete rather than conceptual—of that line from the *Heart Sutra*, "form is emptiness, emptiness is form". Once again it's our concepts, the names we name, that make us think of the world around us as composed of solid, unchanging, literal objects. But if we can see "spaces" as "solid" and "solid objects" as "spaces", then we are momentarily free of concepts; we live in a world of voidness and impermanence, and we ourselves are just as void and impermanent as the world around us is. If we could completely free ourselves from attachment to concepts, from the world of the Monkey Mind, that's how things would appear. (That perceptual seed Lew planted in my psyche sprouted years later, when, meditating with my eyes open in a redwood grove in Gerstle Park in San Rafael, California, the redwood grove was suddenly transformed into a birch grove: the redwood trees, empty; the spaces between them, birch trees.)

THREE

Walking Meditation

In his poem "Wobbly Rock", Lew says:

> On a trail not far from here
> Walking in meditation
> We entered a dark grove
> And I lost all separation in step with the
> Eucalyptus as the trail walked back beneath me...

This is an adjunct to the Buddhist practice of walking meditation. It shouldn't be over-emphasized, but at one point it might help you get deeper into the practice and learn what it has to teach you. Because what you actually see through your eyes while walking is not yourself moving through a landscape, but your feet moving and the ground flowing back beneath them. "Myself moving through a landscape" is an *imagined* image, seen as if by an outside observer; "the trail walking back beneath me" is what you *really* see, right before your eyes. But why don't you immediately recognize that this is what you are seeing? Because the mere *idea* of "here I am walking through a landscape" overwhelms your actual experience. When such extraneous ideas disappear, your perspective changes, and vice versa.

We think of the Earth as stationary and us as scampering around on the surface of it. But we also know that the Earth is turning on its axis, and orbiting the Sun, and the Sun orbiting the center of the Milky Way, and the Milky Way doing God knows what. The Earth is no more stationary than we are—so "moving" and "stationary" are arbitrary concepts, nothing but mental habits. If what is usually taken to be stationary is seen as moving, and what we usually see as moving is experienced as stationary, these habits—some of the most basic and unchallenged perceptual habits we have—are temporarily broken.

The next two of Lew Welch's spiritual exercises are in the form of riddles. Lew composed a set of three riddles, called "The Rider Riddle", "The Riddle of Bowing", and "The Riddle of Hands". I'm leaving out "The Rider Riddle" here because it leads somewhere else, toward Shamanism; it's basically a way of finding your spirit helper or totem beast. But the other two are more like *koans*. They can't be solved by thinking about them; they can only be solved if you let go of all philosophical and symbolic thinking, and make your mind as *concrete* as possible. Lew says about them: "They are Koans for beginners, making no claim for Perfect Enlightenment, but those who solve them will discover a deep spiritual insight." Unlike *koans*, however, they have explicit answers that can be told—but shouldn't; they should only be confirmed if someone gets one right. Each riddle has only one right answer.

As an introduction to these I'll give you the riddle from "Wobbly Rock" along with its solution, just to show you what I mean by "concrete", and to introduce that riddle I need to say (in Lew's words) that Wobbly Rock is "a real rock . . . resting on actual sand at the surf's edge:/Muir Beach, California… Size of the largest hay-stack/It moves when hit by waves/Actually shudders." Lew used to sit on that rock to meditate; it has a precisely square little step or cleft on it that makes a perfect meditation seat (half lotus). I've meditated there myself. (Imagine how sitting in meditation on a huge boulder that clunks back and forth could teach, in a completely visceral, non-conceptual way, *anitya* and *shunyata*.) And—paradoxically—you can only realize the *anitya* part of it, universal motion, if you become *still*—if, as Lew puts it, you "sit real still and keep your mouth shut."

So here's the riddle:

Dychymig Dychymig: (riddle me a riddle)

Waves and the sea. If you
take away the sea

Tell me what it is

This riddle brings together two (not unrelated) things that Lew liked to do: play with language, and point to the world beyond language, the *real* world. The solution is: If you take away "the sea" from "Waves and the sea", you get "Waves and", which, to the ear, is also "wave-sand". So the solution is something anyone who has seen a sandy ocean beach has seen: the pattern of waves, or ripples, left by the ebbing tide in the drying sand. The whole conceptual universe of permanence vs. change, stationary vs. moving, form vs. matter is thus reduced to a single concrete visual image, available to anyone who's ever walked on a sandy beach. Subtract the word-play, and this is precise mind that can solve the following two riddles. (I could add that "The Riddle of Hands" has to do with *jiriki*, "self-power" and "The Riddle of Bowing" with *tariki*, "other-power"— but this is just a later conceptual gloss. It is not a hint but a smoke-screen, a misdirection.)

FOUR

The Riddle of Bowing

In every culture, in every place and time, there has always been a religion, and in every one of these religions there has always been the gesture of bowing so fully that the forehead strikes the ground.

Why is this?

(There is only one right answer to this riddle)

COMMENTARY BY THE RED MONK

Sooner or later the gesture is necessary no matter which way you go. Suzuki bows with so much confidence we all feel bold.

FIVE

The Riddle of Hands

In every culture, in every place and time, there has always been a religion, and in every one of these religions there has always been the gesture of hands clasped together, as Christians do to pray, in order to signify something important.

Why is this?

(There is only one right answer to this riddle)

COMMENTARY BY THE RED MONK:

The gesture has but one source. Who would think to pick his nose, or cross his eyes at such a moment?

The man who claims to feel power between his hands is lost in forms and ideas. The man who clasps his hands and waits will never see the light.

Lew comments: "It is no accident that people, everywhere, have always clasped their hands that way, for those purposes. Think about it. Why not any of the millions of other gestures and stances? Why, always, this one?

"The Riddle of Bowing is much easier of the two. Try that first and use the same Mind to try to solve Hands.

"But please don't waste my time by telling me that Bowing shows respect for the earth or that you are vulnerable to a great power or you are submitting to something. I haven't got time for that baby-talk."

Lew told me the answer to "Bowing", and I solved "Hands" by myself. Whoever wants to crack these riddles must conquer the Monkey Mind and get cured of the Philosopher Disease. Anybody who thinks he or she has solved one or both can apply to me, since I can say "pass" or "fail".

SIX

Looking and Not Looking: Two Half-Koans

I: Suchness

Lew said: "I try to write from the poise of mind that lets me see how things are exactly what they seem."

If things are no different than they seem to be, then they simply are what they are. But if they are just what they are and nothing else, then no *seeming* is involved. And yet, according to Lew, things still "seem". Furthermore, seeing how things *are* exactly what they *seem* requires "poise of mind."

Why is this? (In order to answer this question, try to look at things as if they were exactly what they seem.)

II: Original Face

Lew talked about seeking union with "what goes on whether I look at it or not." It's clear that this kind of union can be based neither on consciousness of the object (since it doesn't depend on *seeing*), nor on a pre-existing identity with the object (since it is something we can *seek*). And it obviously doesn't have to do with stumbling over the object you are looking for in a dark alley.

So—what does it mean to be united with something that goes on whether you look at it or not?

SEVEN

Always In-Between

Lew calls this exercise "Small Sentence to Drive Yourself Sane":

The next time you are doing something absolutely ordinary, or even better, the next time you are doing something absolutely necessary, such as pissing, or making love, or shaving, or washing the dishes or the baby or yourself or the room, say to yourself:

"So it's all come to this!"

This is a *bardo* teaching, debunking (or satirizing) the idea of an end or final resolution in time, such as is commonly represented by the last two big notes of a symphony, or the fairy tale phrase "they all lived happily ever after". *Bardo*, in Tibetan (like the Arabic *barzakh*, "isthmus"), means "in between". It isn't just the time between death and rebirth, but the time between any imagined "beginning" and any anticipated "end", both of which are illusions. We are never just about to reach the happy or the terrible conclusion; we are always in *bardo*. Like Jack Kerouac put it in *Some of the Dharma*, "you just numbly don't get there." *Numbly don't get there* is something we feel when the expected triumph, or disaster, or resolution, turns out to be an anticlimax. But if we don't develop big romantic Kerouacian ideas in the first place, we won't have to feel that numbness; our reaction to the perpetual lack of final closure will change, with practice, from disappointment or impatience into a clear open space... into the Great Silence.

Thus we are always suspended between an imagined beginning and an anticipated end, neither of which are real. If we could really *see* this, we would live in the Present Moment, which is *not* a moment in Time. Like the Cha'an people say, all sentient beings are not to be enlightened *someday*, but "all are enlightened from the beginning"—from the Beginningless.

EIGHT

Art as Nature and Nature as Art

In "Wobbly Rock", Lew writes:

It's a real rock

(believe this first)

Resting on actual sand at the surf's edge:
Muir Beach, California...

Sitting here you look below to other rocks
Precisely placed as rocks of Ryoanji:
Foam like swept stones...

Or think of the monks who made it 4 hundred 50 years ago
Lugged the boulders from the sea
Swept to foam original gravelstone from sea

(first saw it, even then, when finally they
all looked up the
instant AFTER it is made)

Lew finds himself sitting on a rock by the surf; it reminds him of the Zen garden at Ryoanji, made of boulders set in a field of raked white gravel, the gravel meant to suggest the foam of the sea. But in this case the process is reversed: the "real" rock suggests to him the "artificial" rocks, not the other way around. So his mind flips from Nature to Art and back again, from the literal natural rock to the imagined Zen rocks in the famous garden he's only seen paintings of to the actual rock he is sitting on, in Muir Beach, California, all in a split second.

The exercise here, the riddle of it, is: What's the difference between the natural rock *before* it reminds him of the artificial ones (and vice versa), and *after* this happens? It appears to be the very same rock... but is it really?

Lew gives a hint: We only really see anything for the first time— and every act of perception is always "for the first time"—the instant *after* it is made, after we first *make it out*. He goes on:

When I was a boy I used to watch the Pelican:
It always seemed his wings broke
And he dropped, like scissors in the sea...

So he sees the natural bird as if it were an artificial, man-made object. Lew told me that the first time he told that to Philip Whalen, Phil came back with: "But what did you see *before* you saw that?"

NINE

All is Apparition
(Also from "Wobbly Rock")

3 of us in a boat the size of a bathtub . pitching in
Slow waves . fish poles over the side . oars

We rounded a point of rock and entered a small cove...

Clutching to our chip we are jittering in a spectrum
Hung in the film of this narrow band
Green
      to our eyes only...

These lines touch on the central mystery of perception; in Buddhist terms, they make up the teaching of *shunyata* ("voidness") and *tathata* ("suchness")—the truth that things are both void of any ultimate self-nature, and exactly as they seem to be in this moment. (If they possessed suchness without voidness, they would be "objects with egos", opaque and eccentric; if they possessed voidness without suchness they would be nothing but abstract ghosts.) The things of the world are not just fantasies of ours; they go on whether we look at them or not. Yet what little we see of them in no way exhausts them; there is infinitely more to them that what our human eyes and nervous system present to us as "rock, waves, kelp, green ocean water." Things really *are* exactly what they seem; that seeming is not just an image in our brains; the reality of the things we see fills that seeing completely. And yet there is always more to them. As Lew explains elsewhere, in "Four Studies in Perception":

A grove of Laurel grows in the city park.
It grows whether I look at it or not...

But all of it...
Disappears, instantly, if I only look another way.

If I only look another way, I make
Bulldozers, baseball players, and, later
Owls...

It grows whether I look at it or not.
If, as I plan, I wish to chew these leaves and
braid myself a wreath,
I cannot wish the Grove to grow on Taraval Street...

So the practice here is: Try to see the objects of the world as "real things out there", not just scattered parts of yourself, while at the same time realizing that what you see of them, and the way you see them, is something *offered* to you alone. What you "make" of them is neither all there is to them nor some sleepy dream of your own; it is a third thing called an "apparition", a thing that lies beyond the limitations of subject and object. If you could see the world this way, then you would be beyond subject and object too.

If the things we see were only heavy literal lumps, capable of being ignored with impunity because they never really change, then there would be no *tathata*. If what we see were only the act of seeing itself, a made-up pattern woven from fugitive fragments of our own ego, then there would be no *shunyata*. But if things are exactly what they seem, and nonetheless go on whether we look at them or not, then they appear in their full integrity, neither as ignored by the human mind nor as devoured by it. When voidness and suchness are one, the world is both perfectly available to me and perfectly free of me.

See it as so.

❀

The Zen practitioners like to talk about "ordinary mind". Ordinary mind is not, however, the way most people look at the world. It is ordinary, but it is not common; it's probably the rarest thing there is. Ordinary mind is a deep insight into the lessons hidden in the common actions of daily life, and the things we see around us. The spiritual exercises of Lew Welch are designed to help us attend more precisely to these common experiences, and receive their teachings. May they prove fruitful to those who undertake them.

~~14~~

An Exegesis of the
Prologue to William Blake's
The Marriage of Heaven and Hell

Inspired by a Visit to Glastonbury, with an Appendix on the Legend of the Grail

I AM an American poet whose bloodlines flow mostly back to Britain. On a visit to Somerset in 2001, guided there by my British host and hostess who dearly love the place, my British ancestral mythopoetic unconscious was stirred and opened:

> Rintrah roars and shakes his fires in the burdened air

Rintrah, according to S. Foster Damon in his *Blake Dictionary*, is the symbol of God's wrath.

> Hungry clouds swag on the deep.

The clouds are ships of the Royal Navy under full sail, "swaggering" on proud and warlike missions for the Empire; these first two lines are allusions to the atmosphere of the times in which Blake was writing, times of the American Revolution, the French Revolution, and in reaction to them (as David Erdman shows in *Blake, Prophet against Empire*), the suppression of domestic liberties in England, which led to popular protests much like those in America against the Vietnam War; Blake himself was once tried for sedition.

> Once meek and in a perilous path,
> The just man kept his course along
> The vale of death.
> Roses are planted where thorns grow,

152

> And on the barren heath
> Sing the honey bees.

The monks at Glastonbury, where the Thorn grew, and who (as I learned from a friend of our hosts, who served us her rose nectar made according to a monkish recipe) cultivated roses (sacred to the Virgin Mary, the patroness of Glastonbury Abbey), kept to the straight path of salvation, the path of self-annihilation, of death-before-death, in the valley of Somerset, which is identified in legend as the Vale of Avalon, the earthly face of the Celtic otherworld (the hills of Somerset, remember—including the one where the Tor rises—were once islands), and is thus also the vale of death. And monks, like bees, live in *cells*. I myself saw beekeepers in Glastonbury.

> Then the perilous path was planted,
> And a river and a spring,
> On every cliff and tomb
> And on the bleached bones
> Red clay brought forth.

The monks were martyred and planted in their graves, planted only to sprout up again in resurrection—and the bloody spring of Glastonbury (its water so *chalybeate*, so full of iron, that it tastes like blood) is their martyr's blood springing from the ground, reddening (as I saw with my own eyes) with iron rust the little cliff over which it pours, then flowing into Arthur and Gwenivere's tomb—which is directly downhill from the spring—who represent all the dead of England, and the Earth too—in aggregate, Adam the Primordial Humanity, whose name means "red clay". The vivifying blood of the martyred monks raises Arthur from his tomb, who is also Adam (and thus a type of Blake's Albion), clothing his and Gwenivere's bones in living flesh. (There is strife in that tomb; I fear for the day it is opened.)

> Then the villain left the paths of ease
> To walk in perilous paths, and drive
> The just man into barren climes.

If "the perilous path" is the path of religion, then it was King Henry VIII who took the perilous path of declaring himself pope of the English church, and driving the monks, the just men, from their monasteries.

> Now the sneaking serpent walks in mild humility

The priest of the Church of England has now abdicated his spiritual function and become the submissive propagandist for British imperialism, the hypocritical spirit whose wind fills the sails of those "hungry clouds."

> And the just man rages in the wilds where lions roam.

The Holy Spirit, having abandoned King and Church, has gone into the social wilderness to inspire marginalized and wrathful prophets—like Blake himself.

But the resurrection of Arthur is ambiguous, in line with Blake's identification of the Druid religion (Arthur's mentor was Druid Merlin) with vengeance and political oppression, as opposed to the reign of Christ, based on the forgiveness of sins. So if the return of Arthur is the return of Primordial, Adamic Man, it is also the revolt of Pagan Druidism and the cult of the warrior-king against the "just men" of Christianity—a revolt personified by King Henry, which has ultimately led in our time to an almost complete capitulation of the Liberal wing of the Anglican/Episcopal church to Neo-Paganism, including even (in America at least) witchcraft; Grace Cathedral in San Francisco has been host to Pagan rituals. (It is really the standard-bearer in this regard. Not only is today's England probably the most secular nation in history, but the Episcopal Church in the U.S., according to a recent survey, has the largest number of *atheists* of any "Christian" denomination.)

Well are Blake's books called Prophetic! When, in that lyric from his *Jerusalem*, "And did those feet in ancient time/Walk upon England's mountains green?", alluding to the story of Joseph of Arimathea, a tin merchant and uncle of the Virgin Mary according to legend, who is said to have taken the boy Jesus to England on one of his trading journeys, landing near the mines of Somerset, the Vale then being an inlet if the sea—Blake said: "I will not cease from mental fight/Nor shall my sword sleep in my hand/Till we have built Jerusalem/In England's green and pleasant land", he was, in a way, declaring himself a one-man non-Roman Catholic esoteric English counter-reformation.

And the Grail

The Chalice Well at Glastonbury, with its water that tastes like blood, is, precisely, the Holy Grail. The site was reputedly the earliest Christian site in Britain, founded by Joseph of Arimathea, who, according to legend, brought the Grail containing Christ's blood to Glastonbury after the crucifixion; the monks would readily have identified the chalybeate water with the blood of the Savior, who is sometimes called a Fountain of Living Water.

The Chalice Well incarnates the lesser, feminine, psychic mysteries, the return to the "Adamic" state, to the human essence as God created it—the realization of the Earthly Paradise, which Blake called *Beulah*. The Tor on the hill directly above the Well, sacred to St. Michael (as so many islands off the western coasts of France, Britain and Ireland were and are, according to John Michell: the Celtic Hesperides), situated on St. Michael's Ley, is the Vertical Path, the *axis mundi*, a ray of the greater, masculine, Spiritual mysteries which lead to the transcendence of the earthly human state, to Union with God—Blake's *Eternity*. (First Lethe, then Eunoë; first the Earthly Paradise, then the *Paradiso* itself.) St. Michael in his icons is most often pictured carrying a lance—and so the mystery of the pairing of the Grail with the ever-bleeding Lance in the Grail romances, that so exercised Jessie Weston and others, is no mystery: the blood which, like the wine of the Eucharist, mingles with the pure water of the Chalice Well, ultimately comes from Above; the spear of Longinus piercing the side of the crucified Christ, the lance of St. Michael, and the cross itself (like the Tor, and like Blake's engravings of *Jacob's Ladder* and *The Last Judgement*) are renditions of the *axis mundi*, the path which unites the created universe with its unseen Source.

Furthermore, on the border of the Eastern Orthodox Christian icon of Our Lady of Glastonbury are represented several ancient, local Christian saints, one of whom is *St. Kea*. Upon my return to California I consulted Eastern Orthodox lay nun Katherine McCaffrey, a trove of spiritual and historical lore (to whom I brought a vial of water from the Chalice Well) about who these saints were, and she found the story in one of her books that St. Kea was King Arthur's chaplain, who packed Gwenivere off to a nunnery after her adultery with Launcelot and the dissolution of the Round Table. He was Arthur's *staretz* (Russian) his *geronda* (Greek), both of which mean "elder." So he was undoubtedly the same figure as the *Sir Kay* of Sir Thomas Mallory's *Le Morte d'Arthur* and other Grail romances, who was Arthur's *seneschal*, which also means "elder" or "old man." Kea is the Church image, and Kay the knightly or warrior image, of the same man. Sir Kay was a foul-mouthed, vain and curmudgeonly older knight, threatened by the prowess of younger and stronger men; imagine this as the picture that keen young warriors would have had of a pious, admonishing, older Christian monk—St. Kea—in a time when the Christianization of Britain was far from complete.

In 1906 a clairvoyant, Wesley Tudor Pole, had a vision that the Holy Grail was hidden in the Chalice Well at Glastonbury (as many sacred relics might well have been hidden by the monks when Henry VIII attacked and destroyed the Catholic monasteries). The Well was searched, and the searchers discovered therein a small blue glass dish, about six inches in diameter, with flakes of silver embedded in the glass. This is highly interesting in view of the fact that he Grail appears in the *Perceval* romance of Chrétien de Troyes not as a stone or a cup, but as a shallow silver dish, somewhat like the "patten" that is used to carry the consecrated host, or prevent it from falling to the ground. And although it is described as a "dish such as might be used to serve salmon or lampreys"—a large platter, in other words—this may be nothing but a bit of mis-direction to put relic thieves off the track: a dish that carries the Eucharist is thereby carrying *Ichthys*, Christ the Fish, the further implication being that the Fisher King in *Perceval* is actually in need of, and fishing for, Christ. And given that blue is the heraldic color of the Virgin Mary in the Western Christian tradition, and that silver is the Lunar metal and thus the pre-eminent symbol of archetypal femininity, we may conjecture that the dish found in the Well was considered to be an emblem of the Virgin. Gazing upon those flakes of silver embedded in dark blue glass, one is reminded of the starry midnight sky, particularly of the star-clouds of the Milky Way—and also of the star-embroidered cloak of the Virgin of Guadalupe, whose traditional image is the only true *icon* of the Western Church. Thus by all appearances the dish brought up out of the Chalice Well is emblematic of the Virgin Mary as Queen of Heaven.

In the icon of Our Lady of Glastonbury, the Virgin is overshadowed by a smaller figure of St. Michael, bearing the lance. The Virgin holds in her right hand the Glastonbury Thorn and in her left hand the Christ Child, himself carrying a globe of the starry heavens—which may in fact be symbolically equivalent to the Blue Chalice. In time and becoming, Christ Incarnate emerged from the matrix of the Virgin; in Eternity, Christ as God Himself carries her in the hollow of his in His hand, and gazes upon her forever, knowing her as the bearer of the constellations of all the eternal archetypes hidden in His secret Essence.

Esoterically speaking, the Holy Grail is the spiritual Heart, *al-Qalb*: the inviolable center of the human soul, host to the Spirit of God in man, which is the Eye of the Heart—that reality called *Nous* by the Hesychasts and *al-Ruh* by the Sufis, and symbolized in *Perceval* by the Host within the Grail. As the material Grail—if it ever existed—was the vessel that contained the flesh and blood of Christ, either carnally or under the species of bread and wine, so the Spiritual Grail contains both the Knowledge of God (the bread) and the Love of God (the wine). Whoever finds this Grail, and looks upon it with a constant and unwavering gaze, will be fed from it, healed of all his infirmities, and granted the boon of eternal life.

~~ 15 ~~

Hamlet's Soliloquy:
A Metaphysical Exegesis

Excerpted from *Knowings in the Arts of Metaphysics, Cosmology and the Spiritual Path*, Sophia Perennis, 2008

HAVING finally endured enough second-rate Hamlets out-herod-ing Herod, and watched and heard even the greatest Shakespearians defeated by the Soliloquy—Olivier holding irony beneath him, though sublimity was not above him, Burton struggling with it like an anaconda, twisting, lashing out against the teeth of incomprehension—I've concluded that only a metaphysical exegesis can give those words the space they need to fly, without undue torrent, tempest and whirlwind, to their eternally-destined targets:

> To be or not to be,—that is the question:—
> Whether 'tis nobler in the mind to suffer
> The slings and arrows of outrageous fortune,
> Or to take arms against a sea of troubles,
> And by opposing end them?

To battle fate or submit to it, to live on or to sacrifice, or to take, one's life—of course these are embraced by the question Hamlet poses. But the question itself is bigger—so big, in fact, that the questioner, if he be Prince Hamlet of Denmark, is too small to ask it. Hamlet's downfall will not arise out of a wrong answer to the question he poses, but out of the arrogation to *himself* of the right to determine his own existence or annihilation, and the mad belief that he has or ever could have the power. It is God Alone who says what is to be and what not to be, not the puny ego, not the psychic man forgetful of the Spirit, whom Shakespeare beautifully nails elsewhere in the play by having his hero say of himself, "I could be bounded in a nutshell and count myself king of infinite space— were it not that I have bad dreams." The ego that labors under the delusion that it is self-created—the ego that *is*, in fact, *nothing but* this delusion—also believes that it can end itself; if this were only true, hell would hold no terrors.

The arrogant, megalomaniac ego says: To take arms is to be; to suffer is to be annihilated. The contemplative ego says: To suffer is to be, since fortune is the mask of God; to take arms is to be annihilated—because who can fight the Almighty? Who can fight the waves of the sea? Yet the contemplative ego is still an ego; capitulation to fate is still not resignation to the Will of God. What if He orders us to fight? What then? What if the only way we can be annihilated, as ego, is to cross swords with the Unconquerable? As W. B. Yeats says in "The Four Ages of Man":

> He with body waged a fight—
> But body won; it walks upright.
>
> Then he struggled with his heart;
> Innocence and peace depart.
>
> Then he struggled with his mind;
> His proud heart he left behind.
>
> Now his wars on God begin:
> At stroke of midnight, God shall win.

Only the ego is capable of making a distinction between action and resignation, self-being and self-annihilation; they are the loom upon which it is woven. The Spirit of God has never heard of them.

> To die,—to sleep,—
> No more; and by a sleep to say we end
> The heart-ache, and the thousand natural shocks
> The flesh is heir to, 'tis a consummation
> Devoutly to be wisht.

Indeed it is a consummation, and indeed it is to be wished *devoutly*; annihilation in God is, precisely, the consummation of all devotion, the end of the spiritual Path. The ego, however, cannot

know this; the ego's rendition of annihilation in God is mere suicide—that great act of "self-determination"! To the ego, death is a
sleep; to the Spirit, death is the great Awakening. To die in the Spirit
truly is *to die to sleep no more.*

> To die,—to sleep,—
> To sleep! perchance to dream: ay, there's the rub;
> For in that sleep of death what dreams may come,
> When we have shuffled off this mortal coil,
> Must give us pause…

Here the Prince begins to suspect the truth: that to be or not to be
cannot be decided by the ego. And yet, what any normally religious
man can do, this wise fool, this over-sophisticated, self-determined
Renaissance man, this lifelong university student, cannot; he cannot
say: Almighty God, my life and my death are in Your hands. Too
smart to believe that death ends everything, too stupid to realize—
or too proud to admit—that the Almighty holds him in the hollow
of His hand, what else can he do but whine?

> For who would bear the whips and scorns of time,
> The oppressor's wrong, the proud man's contumely,
> The pangs of despised love, the law's delay,
> The insolence of office, and the spurns
> That patient merit of the unworthy takes,
> When he himself might his quietus make
> With a bare bodkin?

Those devotees of a false self-abasement who patiently endure
the destruction of their integrity are spurned indeed, just as Hamlet
is spurned, spurned and beguiled, by his own unworthy philosophy.

> …who would fardels bear
> To grunt and sweat under a weary life.
> But that the dread of something after death,—
> The undiscovered country, from whose bourne
> No traveler returns,—puzzles the will,
> And makes us rather bear those ills we have
> Than fly to others that we know not of?

Indeed the will is puzzled, because the will is intrinsically a servant, and in Hamlet's case—Hamlet standing precisely for modern

western man—it is a servant without a Master. The will's Master is the Intellect, the Nous, the Eye of the Heart—which, to Hamlet, is truly an "undiscovered country," as it must be to anyone who tries to *think with his will*, who neither directly discerns nor faithfully holds to any true Principles outside the will and its mental reflections. The will, blind to the Intellect or else rejecting it (and what else can the blindness of the will be but a *willful* blindness?), can do nothing but bear itself as a fardel, grunt and sweat under its own weariness, and dread the void in which the Spiritual Intellect lies hidden, that land which can only be reached when the ego dies? Truer words were never spoken than that the spiritual traveler never returns from that undiscovered country—and yet one Traveler did. Hamlet, we can now see, though Prince of a supposedly Christian nation, has lost his hold on Christ—and this is a loss that all his modern Renaissance sophistication can never redress. Christ for the Christian is the Way, the Truth and the Life; who has Christ has no right to call life a meaningless burden, and death an undecipherable mystery. Death has been deciphered, and life too; Christ is their exegesis. Yet all that remains of the Kingdom of Heaven in Hamlet's soul is his vague but all-too-valid apprehension that insofar as the other world is undiscovered, it harbors nameless ills—though such ills are truly nameless only to those who have lost the Name.

> Thus doth conscience make cowards of us all;
> And the native hue of resolution
> Is sicklied o'er with the pale cast of thought;
> And enterprises of great pith and moment,
> With this regard, their currents turn awry,
> And lose the name of action.

Thus doth conscience make cowards of us all. What a telling characterization of the psychic man, the mental-willful man, to whom the Spirit, the *pneuma*, can only appear, insofar as it does appear, as a kind of foreknown doom. Hamlet is like a titan who foresees that in the war against the gods the titans will lose, and so gives up the struggle—not in resignation to the Will of God, but in spineless capitulation to the despair of the ego, the source and destiny of the ego's puny pride. True *conscience* is, on the moral level, firm guidance to the will, and on the Intellectual level—the level of *syndere-*

sis—the direct apprehension of spiritual Truth by means of a "knowing together" which marries knower and known in devout consummation—or rather, which reveals the Knower and the Known to have been One in essence from the beginning: "Two distincts, division none: number there in love was slain" [from "The Phoenix and the Turtle"].

Hamlet's "conscience", however, is nothing but the mental reflection of the ego in the warped and shattered mirror of the conditional world, where nothing *must* be because nothing is intrinsically true, where anything *might* be because anything at all might happen—given that the future is an undiscovered country, harboring the ego's perfect shadow, which is fate. Without access, through Intellection, to eternal Truth, thought is precisely *sick*, and integral action impossible. The native hue of resolution is the tincture of the Intellect upon the devout and submissive will, who as a servant bears Its colors; this is *true* conscience, which makes a coward only of self-will, while conferring upon the loyal will, the will which has sworn fealty to It, unerring guidance, legitimate validation, and its true place in the cosmic order. This is the great good fortune of the will that knows a King. For Hamlet, however, the king is a usurper, just as will has usurped Intellect within his own soul; the true King, the Divine Intellect, is dead.

16

The City of Byzantium in the Symbology of William Butler Yeats

AT HIS BEST, at his peak, Yeats was a true metaphysical poet. He approached metaphysics through his studies of Blake and Neoplatonism, as well as through the occultism of the Order of the Golden Dawn, who apparently attempted to revive certain methods of theurgic invocation practiced in classical antiquity. This last influence, which was by no means peripheral to his worldview and his art, might well have classed him among René Guénon's "agents of the counter-initiation", along with his Golden Dawn colleague Aleister Crowley—except for the magnificent use he made of it. In the process of constructing his vast system of esoteric history, eschatology and character-analysis that he titled *A Vision*, based on material channeled through his wife as spirit-medium with himself as amanuensis, he once told the spirits that he would be willing to dedicate the rest of his life to completing and propagating their philosophy—to which they answered: "But no, you don't understand— we have come to give you metaphors for poetry." One might even go so far as to assert that the whole heterodox poison-tree of spirit messages and psycho-occult religion represented by the Theosophical Society and their sister and successor organizations in the 19th and early 20th centuries, including the Golden Dawn, did at last, by the grace of God, bear at least one delicious and nourishing fruit: the poetry of William Butler Yeats. It was as if God could not bring Himself to finally and totally damn a cultural movement, wrongheaded as it might have been, to which the human race had contributed so much of its spiritual aspiration—so he opted to let Yeats sing. It is sad that the salvageable residue of all that often blasphemous psychic mind-play would amount to no more than a few exquisite lyric poems, but it would have been much sadder if those poems had never come down to us.

In his early poem "The Song of Wandering Aengus" the hero, the poet's alter-ego, goes into a hazel wood and catches a "little silver trout". The trout turns into "a glimmering girl, with apple-blossoms in her hair",

> Who called me by my name and ran
> And faded through the brightening air.

The poem ends with Aengus' vow to spend the rest of his life searching for her. It is possible for us to imagine that the elusive "glimmering girl" the poet pulled as a trout from that woodland stream, and who escaped his grasp like the slippery fish she was, later became for him his unattainable muse Maude Gonne—severe through her very refusal to play the role of "severe and unattainable Lady" to Yeats in the mask of "love-struck, petitioning poet". And we may further imagine that even Maude Gonne gave way, late in his life, to his imaginal city of Byzantium, such as it appears in two of his latest and greatest masterpieces, "Sailing to Byzantium" and "Byzantium". This Greek and Christian metropolis—known to the Greeks as Byzantium, to the Christians as Constantinople, and to the Turkish Muslims of today as Istanbul—appears in these poems as a symbol of a final Apollonian spiritual realization, beyond the Dionysian cycles of nature, and thus as the consummation of his life's-work as a poet to whom metaphysics and romance were one task and one reward. As Blake's Jerusalem was the Emanation, and thereby the tantric *Shakti*, of The Giant Albion, so Byzantium became, for Yeats, the completion of a lifetime's spiritual labor appearing before him as a paradisical city of inspired human craft (also reminding of Blake's Golgonooza), strictly comparable the Heavenly Jerusalem of the Book of Revelations.

The first of Yeats' two Byzantium poems has as its theme the Spiritual Path, the road that leads from the "sensual music" of time to the "artifice of Eternity":

Sailing to Byzantium

That is no country for old men. The young
In one another's arms, birds in the trees
—Those dying generations—at their song,
The salmon-falls, the mackerel-crowded seas,
Fish, flesh, or fowl, commend all summer long
Whatever is begotten, born, and dies.
Caught in that sensual music all neglect
Monuments of unageing intellect.

An aged man is but a paltry thing,
A tattered coat upon a stick, unless
Soul clap its hands and sing, and louder sing
For every tatter in its mortal dress,
Nor is there singing school but studying
Monuments of its own magnificence;
And therefore I have sailed the seas and come
To the holy city of Byzantium.

O sages standing in God's holy fire
As in the gold mosaic of a wall,
Come from the holy fire, perne in a gyre,
And be the singing-masters of my soul.
Consume my heart away; sick with desire
And fastened to a dying animal
It knows not what it is; and gather me
Into the artifice of eternity.

Once out of nature I shall never take
My bodily form from any natural thing,
But such a form as Grecian goldsmiths make
Of hammered gold and gold enamelling
To keep a drowsy Emperor awake;
Or set upon a golden bough to sing
To lords and ladies of Byzantium
Of what is past, or passing, or to come.

In the first stanza the natural world of birth and death is identified with the rivers and the sea, the fish within them, and the summer season, thus positing Byzantium and its "monuments of unageing intellect" as the opposite pole, the winter and Northern

165

one, and identifying the city with Hyperborea, the land of eternal spring behind the North Wind where Apollo came from. The North is the point of the Pole Star, "the still point of the turning world" in T. S. Eliot's phrase from *Four Quartets*, the visible point of Eternity in the created order. Dante in the *Purgatorio* placed the polar constellations of the Bears directly above Jerusalem, making that holy city the projection onto the earthly plane of the eternal, celestial order; likewise Yeats with Byzantium.

In the second stanza, those young and dying generations sing the song of *avidya-maya* ("ignorance-apparition"), but old age has a song of its own, one not dependent upon the eros of birth and death but rather upon its deepening identification with the hierophanies of its own eternal archetype—the song of *vidya-maya* ("wisdom-apparition"). And the home of all the archetypes of wisdom is Byzantium, which is to be reached not by sporting or sinking in the sea of material nature, but by surmounting it, sailing upon it, as Christ walked upon the water, driven by the wind of the Spirit.

The third stanza identifies these hierophanies with the sages or iconic saints who have "broken the teeth of time" (cf. Yeats' poem "The New Faces") and thereby become crystallized in their eternal essences. Organic life has a cycle, the cycle of the rivers, the ocean and the rain, but eternity has its own cycle. The holy sages descend and "perne in a gyre" (turn in a spiral) so as to draw their devotee up higher into their world, like Dante on his spiral path up the Mount of Purgatory. The poet asks the sages to consume the natural affections and identifications of the heart that's attracted to nature's sensual music, to alchemically transmute them into the philosopher's stone which is the fruit of the *magnum opus*, the great work of the eternalization of the soul through art, both in line with nature and against it, so as to arrive at that higher nature, eternal and unchanging, beyond decay and death, which Dante rendered in his *Purgatorio* as the Terrestrial Paradise.

In the fourth stanza the poet vows to become eternalized not as any form of nature, but as a form of art in which nature is raised to a higher level by human spiritual labor under the inspiration of God, purged and forged to a gold and enamel artifact in His holy fire. The golden bird is a bird of spiritual vigilance, singing to prevent the Emperor, who is the human mind, from falling into a lethal *amnesia*—"forgetfulness"—by the power of the Platonic *anamnesis*—"remembering" (as in the Greek Orthodox *mnimi Theou*, "remembrance of God")—which is equally *aletheia*, the realization of metaphysical truth pictured as an "unveiling", a notion quite common in the Sufi tradition. Aeneas took the Golden Bough so as to open the gates of Hades, the underworld, and visit his dead father Anchises, leaving it behind as a gift for Persephone. The Golden Bough is identified with the evergreen mistletoe which retains its color unchanged as the tree on which it grows loses its leaves in the Autumn and puts out new ones in the Spring; it therefore stands as a symbol of eternity surmounting time. Thus the alchemical bird, perched on that bough, transcends time as well, which is why he can sing the knowledge of past, present and future.

This is the ideal of the Spiritual Path and the eternal Goal to which it leads; it is a true ideal and well worth pursuing. When Byzantium is actually reached, however, the lyrical announcement of the spiritual traveler's journey and his future apotheosis is transmuted into the existential *agon* of realization, into the Thing Itself. "Sailing to Byzantium" pictures the Lesser Mysteries, the location of the spiritual Center, attractive and fascinating, and the journey toward it, whereas "Byzantium" is all about the Greater Mysteries, and the spiritual death they exact. God's Beauty consummates itself in the encounter with His fiery Majesty; lyric beauty is sacrificed, its blood spilt, so as to as to bring forth a greater Beauty, in which Beauty and Majesty are One: "A terrible beauty is born" [Yeats, "Easter, 1916"]:

Byzantium

The unpurged images of day recede;
The Emperor's drunken soldiery are abed;
Night resonance recedes, night walkers' song
After great cathedral gong;
A starlit or a moonlit dome disdains
All that man is,
All mere complexities,
The fury and the mire of human veins.

167

Before me floats an image, man or shade,
Shade more than man, more image than a shade;
For Hades' bobbin bound in mummy-cloth
May unwind the winding path;
A mouth that has no moisture and no breath
Breathless mouths may summon;
I hail the superhuman;
I call it death-in-life and life-in-death.

Miracle, bird or golden handiwork,
More miracle than bird or handiwork,
Planted on the star-lit golden bough,
Can like the cocks of Hades crow,
Or, by the moon embittered, scorn aloud
In glory of changeless metal
Common bird or petal
And all complexities of mire or blood.

At midnight on the Emperor's pavement flit
Flames that no faggot feeds, nor steel has lit,
Nor storm disturbs, flames begotten of flame,
Where blood-begotten spirits come
And all complexities of fury leave,
Dying into a dance,
An agony of trance,
An agony of flame that cannot singe a sleeve.

Astraddle on the dolphin's mire and blood,
Spirit after Spirit! The smithies break the flood,
The golden smithies of the Emperor!
Marbles of the dancing floor
Break bitter furies of complexity,
Those images that yet
Fresh images beget,
That dolphin-torn, that gong-tormented sea.

The images of day recede—but why "unpurged"? Because this is
the entry into Night, into the Transcendent Darkness, where the
purity or impurity of the conscious spiritual Day becomes irrelevant; in the words of the Book of Revelations (22:11), "let the filthy
be filthy still." The will that could rebel or repent, symbolized by
"the Emperor's drunken soldiery", is now fast asleep, allowing the

Thing Itself, once veiled by the light of the sun, to emerge from its obscurity. In the face of that Thing the noise of Existence, the cathedral gong and the night-song of the town crier—even, that is, the resonance of the creative Divinity and the voice of spiritual vigilance and warning—must be silenced, so that the motionless dome of the Hagia Sophia, the Church of Holy Wisdom, may reflect the Moon and the Stars. The fury and the mire are not purged, only disdained and forgotten.

And what rises next, as herald of the Thing Itself, is one of those images that Yeats spent many years invoking, by virtue of God-knows-what unholy necromancy of a resurrected Paganism, or at least the corpse of it reanimated for a moment in memory of what powers the poets had wielded once in bye-gone ages, summoned back out of *Anima Mundi*, the Soul of the World. This is no holy angel, saint or prophet, but one of the voiceless legions of the dead. What can one like this contribute to the spiritual/alchemical process? Only his definitive, if unwilled, renunciation of life, of all the fury and the mire that drive onwards the process of becoming; dust-dry and with flesh cracked to the bone, he is now beyond all that. Without the slightest longing for it. Undisturbed by it.

If there ever was a "left-hand path", this is it: necromancy in the service of Transcendence! Inconceivable! And certainly not to be recommended. We may wonder, in awe, why God allowed this. Perhaps it was because the poet/magus rapped on the door of that tomb asking not for worldly power, or to possess a beloved woman, or for clues to buried treasure, or to pierce the veil of the worldly future, but one question only: *What lies beyond becoming?* If the Church's easy answer (easy, at least, in the estimation and practice of the time), and even the Yogi's arcane and technical answer, had become implausible and closed to Yeats' generation, obsessed as they were with spirit-mediumship and talking with the dead, then the purity and one-pointedness of the question itself, the *need to know*, was all that remained to them. And because that was the one thing that remained to Yeats as well, nor would he ever let go of it, that gnawing need—at least in his own rare and special case—was answered. Though he had to travel by the sewers and the back alleys, and enter by the tradesman's door, still, by hook or by crook, *he got there.*

169

But what, we must ask, is this "Hades' bobbin bound in mummy-cloth"? I believe that this is most likely a reference to the *Iunx*, the sacred magical spinning top of Hekate, the triple Goddess who is associated with Hades, and sometimes pictured as his wife or consort.

It came to me once, I forget how (by either research or intuition, and most likely by a combination of the two), that the thongs of the *Iunx*, which was made of solid gold and enclosed a sapphire or a piece of lapis lazuli, extended in two opposite directions from the "stem" or axis of that object. If the *Iunx* (from which we get our word "jinx") were wound in a counter-clockwise direction, wrapping both thongs around the stem, and the thongs were then pulled apart in opposite directions (one in held in each hand), the *Iunx* would spin clockwise. The momentum of this clockwise spin—relatively powerful in a heavy gold object—would then draw the thongs together and wrap them around the stem once again, this time in a clockwise direction, so that when the thongs were pulled apart for the second time, the *Iunx* would now spin in the opposite direction, counter-clockwise. So the spin had four phases to it: clockwise with thongs unwinding, clockwise with thongs rewinding, counterclockwise with thongs unwinding, and counterclockwise with thongs rewinding. The clockwise spin undoubtedly symbolized, and invoked, *proödos*, the unwinding of the hidden potentials of things into visible space and time, and the counter-clockwise spin, *epistrophe*, the return of all manifested things to the Night of the Unseen, each phase including a period of expansion alternating with one of contraction. (*Proödos* and *epistrophe* strictly correspond to the Vedantic doctrine of the Day and Night of Brahman, the periodic manifestation and dissolution of the universe.) The contraction of *proödos* ended with an *enantiodromia*—a pause and reversal of direction—which began the expansion of *epistrophe*, while the contraction of *epistrophe* ended with a second *enantiodromia* that began the expansion of *proödos*. The pause between *epistrophe* and *proödos* undoubtedly corresponded to the Winter Solstice, that between *proödos* and *epistrophe* to the Summer Solstice, the point where the thongs were most fully unwound during the clockwise phase to the Spring Equinox, and the corresponding point during the counter-

170

clockwise phase to the Autumnal Equinox. So the *Iunx* represented, and also enacted, the entire cosmic process of creation and destruction, spinning about the *axis mundi*, the still point (or vertical shaft) of the turning world. As such we may identify it with the *sangsara* ("whirlpool") of the Buddhists, and also with the *Shakti* and *Mahamaya* of the Hindus, the divine power of manifestation-that-veils (*avidya-maya*) and reintegration-that-reveals (*vidya-maya*), turning about the adamantine point of the Absolute Witness, the *Atman*. (For more on the *Iunx* as a sacred top and the *Iunges* as whirlpools of cosmic manifestation, see Algis Uzdavinys, *Philosophy and Theurgy in Late Antiquity*, a book that I was privileged to edit.)

The same clockwise/counterclockwise representation of *proödos* and *epistrophe* was undoubtedly the symbolic significance of the "scroll" ornament on the capital of the Ionic column. As for the gold body of the *Iunx*, this symbolized the Divine Intellect or Spiritual Sun, identified with *Nous* or Pure Being, while the sapphire or lapis lazuli it enclosed represented the Blue Sky, symbol of the Formless Absolute or Beyond Being, the Matrix out of which the Sun of the Intellect proceeds. (Among the Native Americans, the Cheyenne have the identical symbolism.) And that blue stone was placed in the center of the golden ball instead of surrounding it to indicate that the transcendent inner core of the Intellect is the Formless Absolute itself.

So what is wound up in the process of dying, as the many forms of the daytime world fade and converge into a single Darkness, is simultaneously unwound in the next world, the next *aeon*, so as to manifest all that's hidden in that Darkness. What is concealed by life is revealed by death; likewise what is hidden in death is made manifest in the life to come. If the consummation of the Spiritual Path is, in the words of the Prophet Muhammad, to "die before you die", then the invocation of the dead, the contemplation of the white skull already there, grinning, beneath the living skin, as a way of meditating on death's universality—as the Sufis and the Yogis will meditate and pray in graveyards or the Tibetans drink from cups made out of human skulls—may aid in the work, as the Sufis put it, of becoming "like a corpse in the hands of a Washer of the Dead". According to the Sufis, the final two phases of this process of dying before you die are '*Fana*, Annihilation in God—"death in life"—and *Baqa'*, Subsistence in God—"life in death".

And the form this final Subsistence takes is, once again, the Artificer's golden bird, crowing its bitter triumph over the regime of ever-birthing, ever-dying, ever-turning Nature, the lower "sublunary" world ruled by the cycles of the Moon, in which everything is always becoming but nothing can ever *be*. And that bird, formed of the eternal and incorruptible Gold of the Intellect, in crowing, awakens the cocks of Hades, who herald the coming of the dawn in the underworld—the Resurrection of the Dead. Those flame-begotten flames, flitting at night on the Emperor's pavement, are shades out of Hades in the first stages of resurrection and transmigration, on their dark, purgatorial way to rebirth as fully-living spirits capable of populating Paradise. The effect of their dance, and the agony of their trance, is to purge themselves of the complexities of organic, created life, so as to become *simple* like the angels are—each angel, according to Thomas Aquinas, being formed on, and manifesting the light of, a single Idea.

The eternal spirits, sown broadcast by the Divine Word of Creation, are whirled through the chaos of created nature, the regime of the three-fold Mother Goddess of Crete, in the sea where the dolphins play, swept on and away by the torrent of becoming. But the *smithies*, those laboratories and oratories where the alchemical, supremely *artificial* work of spiritual transmutation is carried on, break that flood of becoming, and return those exiled spirits, as tribute, to the audience halls of the Emperor—who is *Christos Pantocrator*, Christ the King. In the marble mosaic of His dancing-floor are set the archetypal patterns that transform the welter of chaotic change that characterizes the world of becoming—driven on by the suffering of matter in exile from the Spirit—into a formal dance. This is the true function of art when recognized as spiritual labor, of art in the Thomistic/Aristotelian sense such as Dante understood it: namely, that Divine function which constellates and harmonizes *materia* by the transcendent power of *forma*, thereby transforming Potency into Act. The great cathedral gong, symbol of the vibratory radiance of the Logos, summons those spirits riding the backs of dolphins to arise from the turmoil of life—and that same gong *cre-*

ates the very turmoil out of which it calls them. The identical *Fiat Lux* that initiates the oceanic turbulence of the natural world, with all its torment, simultaneously summons the life-principles of that world to shake themselves loose from it, arise from it, and return to the transcendent, vibratory Center of the Word that made them— to the Spirit of God that moves on the face of the waters.

So I guess we can forgive Yeats his bit of latter-day necromancy, his anachronistic Neo-Pagan mumbo-jumbo, seeing that "by their fruits ye shall know them!" Because, certainly and without doubt, the man found what he was looking for. If "in dreams begin responsibilities" [epigraph to Yeats' book *Responsibilities*], I say he fulfilled the task laid upon him by the Great Artificer that he sang in these two magnificent poems—a task that was written down for him before he ever drew breath in this world. By his greatly-conceived and triumphantly-concluded labor, he is certainly fit to "dine, at journey's end/With Landor and with Donne" [from "To a Young Beauty"]—and with Blake and Dante too.

❧ 17 ❧

Seeing God

You saw Yourself in my mirror
Clearly, with no admixture of other-than-You—
Yet as I watched You in the act of that seeing,
Eavesdropping from an inch above Your shoulder,
Your image had just barely a touch, just barely the
    shadow
Of the sly look of "me" in it…
I saw both that You saw Yourself perfectly,
And that I myself could not see in that way…
So, You tell me: Did I see You, or not?

But the truth is, I don't need You to tell me;
Strictly speaking, for me to ask You to confirm a
    realization of mine
Is the height of discourtesy.
All that I need is for You to see me,
As You most certainly see me even now;
All that I ask is that You make me perfectly content
    only to be seen by You—
And if You make me see that I am seen,
    I know I *will* be content.
May you be equally content with me,
Until I see You again.

☙ 18 ☙

Watching Olivier's *Lear*

Excerpted from *Knowings in the Arts of Metaphysics, Cosmology and the Spiritual Path*, Sophia Perennis, 2008

LEAR AS KING is the *Nous*, the Eye of the Heart, the One Self at the Center of all. "The soul is an aristocrat," said Meister Eckhart. Lear uncrowned is the ego—"Lear's shadow" as the fool now calls him. Lear-as-ego believes that the love and fealty granted Lear were granted him as ego, not as King. He wants to be loved for his "self" alone, not for his golden crown. But his golden crown *was* that Self. "Not for their own sakes are father, child, lord, vassal, beloved loved, but for the sake of the Self," the Hindu scriptures declare.

The ego believes it can reign without ruling, that to be taken for a King by others—the image of a King, a player King—is to be "every inch a King": not that the Real plays at existence, but that the play itself is real. So *Laila*, the Divine Play, becomes *Maya*. The ego veils, denies, rebels against the Self, and then expects to retain all the Self's prerogatives. But this can never be. When the crown passes from the Self to the ego, who immediately loses it, or throws it away, the faculties of the soul rebel. *Gon*-eril (lust) and *Reg*-an (the power motive) now divide the kingdom; *Cord*-elia (the Heart) is banished, murdered. Thus the Golden Age becomes senile; Manawyddan ap Llyr may no longer drive his chariot over the waves of what Blake called "the Sea of Space and Time" as if it were a flowering meadow; Christ no longer walks upon the Sea of Galilee in the sight of men. Man falls; the Golden Age ends. This Shakespeare, living through his own lesser fall—the end of the Middle Ages in England, the late northern birth of the Renaissance, the discovery of nature, of history, of the Empire of the Ocean Sea, of man bounded in a nutshell, counting himself king of infinite space, and beset by bad dreams— well knew; well knew.

～19～

The Curse of Poetic Subjectivism

POETRY has nothing to do with self-expression. What begins with "myself", considered apart from the rest of reality, also ends with myself. And what begins and ends with myself can be of no real interest to anybody else, nor will it necessarily be of much interest to me either; if it is possible for me to bore or disgust others, it is equally possible for me to be bored and disgusted in my own presence. And to the degree that I remain sealed within my own particular concerns, obsessions, tastes, hankerings and fixed ideas, unwilling to grant the authority and dignity of authentic being to anything outside myself, then boredom and disgust—and also fear—will most likely be my companions. Poetry, unless we include childish fantasy and incoherent mumbling ("language poetry" for example) in the definition of it, exists to express *truths*. A truth is something that, in the words of Beat Generation poet Lew Welch, "goes on whether I look at it or not." There are truths of the metaphysical world, truths of the natural world, truths of the human world, even truths of the emotional and psychological state and configuration of the poet him- or herself. But even when the poet is writing *about* himself, he is not writing *as* himself, at least not in the biographical sense. Unless his own states have become as objective to him as the facts of history or the stars in the sky, he'd better keep his mouth shut.

In some ways poetry is the end of the line—the line being the creative act of God. God brings forth the universal order; inspired by the exalted archetypes and constants of that order, and in some cases under the direct inspiration of God Himself, the poet creates. Moved by the meanings and ironies, the joys and tragedies of human life, or by the beauties and terrors of the natural world, all of

176

which spring from these primary archetypes, the poet creates. Intrigued by the drama of human history, its triumphs and its crimes—which also reflect the actions of God, both His mercy and His wrath, both His guidance and His dark misdirection of those who reject that guidance—the poet creates. True to the existential reality of his or her own experience, its precise qualities beyond all conceptual overlay and analysis, the poet creates.

Or does he? Has not God already created everything? Is He not the Creator of all things visible and invisible, both of all the words human beings have said, and all the numberless things that no-one has ever said, or even thought of? The world, human society, our bodies, our ability to think and feel, all these come to us as gifts—or as curses—from a Source that absolutely transcends us; even the atheist, if he or she is honest, must admit this much. So the poet can in no way be a creator in the same sense that God is, or even a "co-creator", as if God were in need of partners and helpers to achieve His ends. The poet, if anything, is a *sub*-creator, one who creates not by deepening and expanding being, like God does, but rather by picking and choosing from what That One has already provided so as to express and apply His bounty in more limited and specific worlds. And by the time the universal creative impulse has descended as far as human words, and crossed the lips, tongue and teeth of the poet, it has nowhere else to go—nowhere but back, through the response of the listener—and up, after that, through a thousand unknown listeners in invisible worlds—to the Source that first released it.

Kierkegaard posited three ontological levels, in descending order of reality: the spiritual, the moral and the aesthetic. Human words may praise and characterize and petition and invoke the Divine; this is the spiritual level. They may also motivate human action in the name of a moral ideal, or prohibit actions that violate this ideal; this is the moral level. Lastly, they may simply render the perceived qualities of things, of the objects of the world, of the innumerable states of human consciousness and affection; this is the aesthetic level. Below the aesthetic, below the sensual or affective surface of things, nothing remains but the inarticulate, the inchoate, the obscure. Situated on the lowest level of the hierarchy of being, the aesthetic is perfectly situated to reflect the highest; the bare existential confrontation with the qualities of existing things may suggest the bare contemplative encounter with the names and qualities of God and the metaphysical order, and the Ground of Being itself. Nonetheless, the aesthetic apprehension of already-existing things is situated at the furthest ontological point from the Divine Reality that the world of form allows for. The poet is balancing on the brink of non-entity; if he falls, he is lost. And his only way of avoiding this fall is for him to dedicate his art, even though it is ontologically situated at the opposite pole from Primal Reality, to the contemplation and expression of the truths this Reality both conceals and reveals. He or she need not do this in specifically religious or metaphysical terms; all that is required is that the poet, having gazed into the abyss of non-entity, now turn his or her poetic attention in exactly the opposite direction, toward the point from which everything is arriving, not the point into which everything is departing and disappearing.

T.S. Eliot, in his important essay "Tradition and the Individual Talent" sees pure self-expression in poetry either as a drawback or as something that can be significant only if the poet's "self" embraces, and takes place in the context of, the poetic history of his tribe, a history which informs him and which he also contributes to; this history is an objective fact to which the individual poet, no matter how innovative he finally becomes, can and must relate. Eliot says: "No poet, no artist of any art, has his complete meaning alone. His significance, his appreciation is the appreciation of his relation to the dead poets and artists. You cannot value him alone; you must set him, for contrast and comparison, among the dead." Here "the dead" stand in, at least in part, for the metaphysical order, even though Eliot informs us that he has intentionally stopped short at the threshold of that order. (This reticence certainly does not apply, however, to his studied masterpiece, the *Four Quartets*.) The poets of the "Objectivist School"—Louis Zukovsky, George Oppen, Charles Reznikoff, Carl Rakosi, Kenneth Rexroth and others, whose first progenitor was probably William Carlos Williams— also emphasize historical and social objectivity as the basis for true poetry, through more from a Marxist standpoint than Eliot's quasi-royalist one. And both the Symbolist and the Imagist schools (or streams) of poetry work to free the poem from the subjective limitations of the poet's "biographical" humanity. The *image*, inner or outer, whether it springs from the dream state or from contemplation of the natural world or from some even higher source, is simply *there*, an objective factor that must be dealt with. It is not in essence an expression of the poet's personality; if it falls to this level it remains obscure and unformed, it never fully appears. The same can be said for the *symbol*, since all true symbols are expressions of orders of reality higher than the psychological or the linguistic. Symbols are polyvalent, capable of more than one objectively valid interpretation, because they are supercharged with meaning, greater and subtler and denser meaning than any matter-of-fact statement can carry, no matter how complex, ornate or embellished; and this is not an easy concept for some people to grasp. Certain literalists, when confronted with the polyvalent exegesis of a given symbol, will falsely assume that the exegete has "read those meanings into it", that he is treating the symbol as if it could mean anything he wants it to, as if it were no more than an expression of his subjective habits and predilections. Nothing could be further from the truth. Any symbol will generate a hermeneutic, a specific set of interpretations, that is as objective as the findings of a physical scientist who uses the experimental method to ask questions of the material world. The atomic number for gold is 79 and nothing else; all other answers to the question "what is the atomic number of gold?" are simply wrong. Likewise any interpretation of a symbol that falls outside the set of its objectively valid, intrinsic meanings is, for all the polyvalence a given symbol may exhibit, also wrong. Nonetheless a symbol, unlike an allegory, cannot be translated into a single literal meaning, though literalists believe that it can. They will take whatever one-dimensional literal meaning the symbol suggests to them as its *real* meaning, as if symbolism were nothing more than a game of hide-and-seek poets like to play to make things more interesting, a kind of cipher that need only be deciphered to be understood—but that's not how it is; it is conceivable that a virtually infinite number of meanings might be legitimately drawn from a single symbol. There are, however, different *orders* of infinity, like those found in mathematics. The mathematician Georg Cantor discovered that not every mathematical infinity is infinite in every sense, and that some infinities are "denser" than others; consequently a given infinity does not necessarily embrace *all* infinities, unless we specifically posit an order of infinity that is infinite in every sense—a definition that can only be satisfied by the Deity. Cantor called these limited infinities "transfinite numbers", believing that they had been revealed to him directly by God. (At this point it would also be good to remember that Edgar Allen Poe considered poetry and mathematics to be sister arts, and that the famous Sufi poet Omar Khayyam was also an influential mathematician.) Likewise, though a symbol may give rise to an indefinite set of valid interpretations, since its experienced meaning varies according to who is contemplating it and the contemplator's state of consciousness at any given moment, other sets of interpretations are simply wrong, since they are poetically impossible. A symbol, though it may be refracted into a virtually infinite set of subjective impressions, is a reality in which all the impressions it is capable of producing already exist, prior to manifestation, in a unified synthesis. And it cannot be just anything you want it to be; it is an objective factor with its own specific form, quality and limit.

At the opposite pole from Eliot's view in "Tradition and the Individual Talent" lies Michael McClure's poem "Hymns to St. Geryon, I", the classic expression *poetry as act*; here are two excerpts from it:

I mean that I love myself which is an act of pride
and I would decorate myself with what is beautiful.
The tigers of wrath are wiser than the horses of instruction.—
means that the belief of something is necessary to its beauty.
Size, numbers, are part of any aesthetic. I must
believe my gesture. Beauty fades so quickly

That it does not matter. Belief, pride,—remain.
AND   AND   AND   AND   AND   AND   AND

the gesture.
The mark of the strong shoulder and hand.

The Curse of Poetic Subjectivism

❖

It is hard to avoid some issues.
　The poem could easily become a body,
with elbows, lymph systems, muscles.
　But how ugly! How much better for it

to be a body of words.
A POEM — NO MORE
(Not a body of words but a poem)

I am the body, the animal, the poem
is a gesture of mine.

Here it seems as if the poem has become inseparable not only from the poet himself but even from his body—specifically his youthful body, from the days when McClure was a good-looking young stud addicted to body-building, not an eternal bank-clerk like Eliot was. Yet this poem does not give the impression of being sealed inside somebody else's boring, or even possibly interesting, subjectivity. It lives out in the free air; it is much more a gesture swiftly freed, in the act of it, from the one making it, like any free, powerful, genuine, and integrated gesture must be, than merely some gripe or whine or tremolo rising out of somebody *else's* sleepy or petulant or acerbically self-enclosed self. When I read that poem out loud, the *body* is no longer Michael McClure's; it is mine. The poem enters my body like the air filling my lungs, and when it is shaped and released by the power of the energy it transmits, it moves my body this way and that, just as if the postures I assume and the gestures I make were an integral part of it, almost like implicit stage directions—or like the stylized *mudras* and the cho-reographed, moving postures (knows as *kriyas*) experienced by the Hindu tantric yogis, symbolic gestures that arise spontaneously whenever the human psycho-physical nervous system labors and dances under the influence of Divine-manifestation-as-Power—of *Shakti*. And is not the Muse herself a true shape of *Shakti*?

McClure's poem, and his poetics, are certainly flirting with the kind of narcissism that has made poetry an almost hated art in the contemporary western world; in the title he literally canonizes Geryon, the monster of deception and hypocrisy from Dante's

181

Inferno, a beast with the face of an honest man and the tail of a scorpion, calling him *Saint* Geryon. This is not a good sign. Pride may be beautiful at the moment of its birth, but a middle-aged pride stinks to high heaven. Metaphysically speaking, the problem with McClure's stance is that it casts the poet as the *Shaktiman*, the Power Holder, the Master of *Shakti*—but the truth is, only God is the Holder of Power; when the individual human form assumes that role, this indicates that it is under the power of *Maya*. In the Hindu Tantra, God as the Master of *Shakti* is personified as Shiva, Lord of the Dance, the Formless Absolute, the emblem of pure Consciousness. But insofar as Shiva partakes of form through this very personification, the day comes when He is transformed from the Power-Holder into the slave of the very Power he once held; in Hindu iconography this is pictured as the dance of sword-bearing Kali upon Shiva's prostrate form.

And if a poem can be compromised by the individual narcissism of the self-dramatizing ego, the same can certainly be said for the ponderous pontifications of the superego, the proud and stony identification not with the universal order—divine, natural, or human—but with the *established* order. This is why it would be a good thing for any poet wishing to avoid both *hubris* and stiltedness to study Eliot and McClure together, and then see what he or she comes up with.

Suffice it to say that if the aspiring poet can make a fertile synthesis between the willingness to *speak for oneself*, to bear the burden of creativity and fully accept the consequences of it, and the understanding that only God possesses the right and the power to speak *intrinsically*, not by virtue of a Divine gift, the return of which may required at any moment, then he or she has accepted the existential dilemma inseparable from the role of "poet".

One of the most gratifying compliments that any poet can receive is: "You said exactly what I would have said if I had known how; you spoke not instead of me, but *for* me"; thus a true corollary of *vox populi vox dei* may in fact be *vox poetae vox populi*. If the poet does not know, because he has not been able to confront, the sentiments and convictions, the challenges and delegated works, the enemies and allies, the wounds and imperatives of his own soul, he cannot speak with authority to move, inform and illuminate others; he can never reach any kind of authenticity because he is no *author*. Yet if he does not recognize the *Mysterium Tremendum* in the Cave of his Heart as the First Author and Speaker of all things, including the single soul he must now turn to so as to find his proper matter and form, then he is no author either, only a thief. He is a thief who has stolen a subtle and magnificent device containing untold knowledges and destinies and warfares—things he must redeem from that clenched and paralyzed untoldness precisely by *telling* them—but stolen it in total ignorance of what that device is, what it is capable of, and the skills he must acquire to put it to proper use, the result being that he simply hammers it down to its component parts so he can sell it for scrap.

But if we know that God sees us, then we can see; if we know that God speaks, and that we ourselves are one of His infinite words, unique and never to be repeated, then we can speak.

20

Every Man (or Inch) a King

The democrat struggles with the world,
The aristocrat with himself, said Yeats.
So, do I got a blue-blood side to my character?
Damn straight!

The demo is sentimental,
The aristo, passionate, said that passionate Irishman.
My soul is the rebellious kingdom
I battle to subdue.

That's why it's always better
For the aristocrat to be
Without worldly power. Disinherited.
"The soul is an aristocrat", Meister Eckhart said.

You can't govern a kingdom
Till you can govern yourself,
And you can't govern yourself
Till God takes the Throne—which is your Heart.

Die before you are made to die,
O Anachronism!
Die in single combat!
Throw away the crown!

[NOTE: "Every man a king" was the rallying-cry of the Louisiana populist politician Huey Long, the North American Juan Perón, while "every inch a king" was how Lear described himself in his madness. As for "throw away the crown", the ego throws it away through heedlessness, but the Human Form in the presence of God throws it away through sacrifice. "Throw away the crown" is a phrase from the Yoga tradition; it means: "When the *kundalini* has risen to the *sahasrara* or thousand-petalled lotus at the crown of the skull, don't hold on to that highest experience: relinquish it." When spiritual elevation is achieved and then sacrificed, the Presence of God descends into the Cave of the Heart, the *hrdayam*, and is unveiled as the *Atman*, the Universal Witness. After that, *wherever you turn, there is the Face of God* (Q. 2:115).]

184

21

High Energy Declamatory Verse:
An Excerpt from *The Wars of Love*

MY WORK in the form I have named "high-energy declamatory verse" is probably all that gives my poetry whatever real distinction it might have. It's what I most wanted to do and what I've probably done best, though I have been able to produce only a small amount of it. My short epic *Panic Grass* (1968) is an example of it, as is the excerpt from my second epic, *The Wars of Love* (2011), that appears below. Allen Ginsberg once described my poetry as "manic gibberish", to which I answered, "I would rather call it *intellectual* manic gibberish—admittedly a difficult genre." (The word *mania*, remember, though it usually refers to a pathological psychic condition, can also denote the "divine" madness of the prophet—in Greek, the *mantis*.) Other examples of high-energy declamatory verse include certain passages in Milton's *Paradise Lost*, the "prophetic books" of William Blake as well as his "A Song of Liberty" that concludes *The Marriage of Heaven and Hell*, Allen Ginsberg's *Howl*, some of Michael McClure's poems, Walt Whitman's "A Passage to India", Jalalluddin Rumi's *Divan i-Shamiz i-Tabriz*, and the King James version of the Book of Isaiah. I conclude with this excerpt since it embodies several of the themes I've treated in this book: mythopoesis; the synthesis of logopoeia, melopoeia and phanopoeia; the symbol as representing a higher order of synthetic particularity than the world of "facts" etc. Here it is:

> In the Cave of the Heart shines a hot, interior Sun.
> Sometimes it is veiled by leaden clouds,
> Sometimes by a mist of dull, tarnished gold.
> At times the clouds are a muddy olive color;

185

What Poets Used to Know

At other times, the color of dried blood.
But beyond the veils of despair and complacency,
Of shapeless intoxication and grim spiritual will
A find gold Sun is roaring with knowledge
Over an incandescent ocean, heaving in mountains of divine
    energy,
The tidal-waves of the Aeons: passing as we watch them
But eternal in the Core of radiance, before whose face
We rise, and pass, like voices. Whatever word is heard in that
    light
Stands like a pillar
Between earth and sky.

So now the Violet Fear and the White Fear.
Now the full Beast driven from the heart, rising in front of us,
And us knowing him.

Open Hell. Seal not the door where evil dwells.
Stir the banked coals, the immemorial anger, the mirror-bound
    suicides,
Lizards on a red cliff at dawn . . . they flex the sinews of their
    wings,
They take delight in their own beings. . . .

I say all will be pressed into service.
I say all will be required to fight.
The passive, the coward, the innocent will be trampled down,
Unless locked in single combat with Antichrist
In mountain solitude and stillness.

Invoke, therefore, the war in your marrow;
Call on the fight you were born with, that enemy
Whose lie is cut and tooled, precisely,
To cover your single truth.
Pick targets. Each man is alone with all men
In this night of war. The conglomerate form of Death
Stands guard on each human door,
Solid to the bullet, and the chisel—like those cliffs in the Sinai
In which our skirmishers discovered, still living
The imprisoned forms of men!

An Excerpt from The Wars of Love

The sky is roofed with machines now, a guarded perimeter to
    block out the angelic orders;
The earth is filled with the limbs of struggling giants, locked
    apart in separate mirrors, in cold branching corridors of time;
They are powers of creation chained in elemental caverns when
    the Human Form was planted on earth,
Because Man, when he fell, needed ground under his feet, the
    bedrock of God—
But we have forgotten God now, and the rock is unsteady; our
    foundations crack like parchment, they heave and shift like
    water;
The mechanical chatter of demons, the acid of shattered images
    are our gods and our protectors;
The wasp and the locust advise us; the spider and the scorpion
    guard our sleep.
Who knows this? Who has the courage not to worship
At the feet of his own destroyers?
Friends, I know you.
You are those scourged by what you see in the crackle and hiss
    of fire
That flowers in the rift of God. You have incontrovertible reason,
    proof to silence laughter.
You are the face of the Divine Humanity driven to the margins and
    borders of the Earth,
Weighted and crushed by the Trust, till you release the burden of
    your heavy word, to the pavement, to the center of the Earth
    if necessary
That the heart give up her dead;
You walk through the cities of the grave in the high mountains
    with food and intelligence for your people;
You open your throats to the Messengers to give them a living
    voice; saints take council beneath your ribs;
You offer your bodies to be the purgatory
Of souls you will never know.
You are those who in your hunger did not ask for food and so
    became storehouses;
Who in thirst did not cry for water and so became rivers;
Who in nakedness did not flinch under shame, but suffered it,
    rejecting the cloth of the world,
And so became a city for all people, where no-one is refused

But only those who know how to place their foreheads on the
    dusty earth
Can enter.

You live in that Year
When each man and woman picks up their whole cross and walks,
In the terrible sunrise, down the burning road,
As the structure of consensus reality crashes all around us,
Torn free from the flesh of memory,
Stripped naked to Mercy,
Gone beyond Death—

The scythe reaps, the seed-heads fall
The harvest barn is hidden everywhere in the fire;
And the wedding-smoke rises,
Perfume of all love and murder,
Heroism, quite secret work
In the caverns of the heart,
Pounding the stone doors
Of those sacrificial priests
Who desecrate the Human Form to build the regime of Antichrist,
Gods of the New World Order,
Powers of frigid glamour, and insane false hope, and numb
    despair:
Pour fire against their sanctuary,
Against the Dragon
Against the Tower—
Glyphs of destiny, strung like nets
Through the charged structure of the thunderhead
Weave lightning into working knowledge,
Where the Living Truth sits mounted and armed
In the region of the Air, on the borders of the next world now
    shining into this one, in dream and vision more solid than a
    rock in the hand,
To overturn their altars, those blissful devotees, worshippers of
    despair incarnate
To whom Love is a torturing fire.
At the precise point where their pain and loss are most deeply
    denied,
In the mouth of their wisest wound these words are engraved

An Excerpt from The Wars of Love

White fire cut on black fire on the
Skeletal plasm of their nerves:
And Love is what we wish them.
But how can they accept such a gift from the likes of us?
How can they even know their need?
They are inheritors of the whole world—we are nothing
But inheritors of the earth.

The horn of remembrance now cracks the shell
Encrusted on the heart for six thousand years,
Awakening the nations of the human dead
From their iron sleep. The people of the tombs arise and have
    their say
On the plains of Akhirah:

           "We are those
Who lie slandered under the name of death.
We have incontrovertible reason,
Proof to silence laughter.
From palaces of torture,
From twenty terms in the grey, damp, infinite dusk
We raise our voices and salute you,
Who still sit laboring in your dream—
You living men and women, clothed as we were
In the sweetness and the dignity
Of human flesh. We are the strength of your arms and your loins,
The voice of your living memory.
Speak us, man! Tell our story.
We've been muttering too long in our ruined halls, those narrow
    beds,
The groves still barren of our voices;
We've lain too long in the seed-houses, the uneasy archives,
    the crucibles of sleep.
Beware! The dead are hungry for those who will not live;
The ones who die into a coward's dream we consume;
We eat, and are not satisfied.
But as you remember Him, He will also remember us, in our
    chambers of darkness

189

Till the river of our endless dying flows East again,
Toward the rising sun."

    If the instinct to seek news of higher realities and to see the things of this world in light of them can be called "romantic", then this is romantic poetry. (Sister Mary Norbert Körte understood this when she told me, back in the 60's: "Charles, you are not a Beat poet.") We now reject the romantic sensibility as foolish idealism, incompatible with the horrors of the modern world. Yet it is still possible to contemplate even a world like this—one characterized by vast psychic and material devastations on the collective level, the personal level, and what might be called the "molecular" level—from a higher ontological standpoint, without in any way rejecting the "cold hard facts". It is my belief, however, that in our time the romantic sensibility can only be fully rendered through the genre of apocalypse.

❧ APPENDIX ❧

Occidental Poetics:
A Vindication of Spiritual Idealism

by Jennifer Doane Upton

TRADITIONALLY poetry has been a vehicle for bringing the eternal dimension of things into collective consciousness; this is the archetypal use of the art. Many contemporary poets, however, aren't interested in following this archetype. They tend to rely on their talent alone, rather than the intrinsic truth of their subject, because they have become infected with the contemporary delusion that talent is paramount and sufficient unto itself. But to exclusively rely upon skill or talent is always to serve the established worldview, the spiritual status quo. The poet who takes this road may *feel* creative, but the truth is that he or she is only involved in imitation.

Since intrinsically spiritual values are at odds with our collective mind-set, poets who devote themselves to such values nowadays often feel like outcastes. To find and express a deeper and more exalted worldview than the common level of things is a difficult step—one that few people are willing to attempt because they feel that their lives are already difficult enough. But sometimes the only way to overcome a difficulty is to embrace it.

Poets who work with deep or exalted subjects are ultimately trying to show us the final goal of the spiritual life, since without a true vision of that goal we will find neither the motivation nor the insight necessary to attain it. This vision can be dangerous, however—especially if it convinces us that we've already arrived at that goal, when in reality we have not. If we fall for this illusion we will become imbalanced and spiritually inflated, which will block our

191

progress on the path just as effectively as despair or spiritual blindness. This is why the vision of divine realities must be grounded in labor and sacrifice. Dante Alighieri grounded his vision of spiritual sublimity, and prevented it from generating imbalances, by first taking the reader through Hell—and he could not have done this if he himself had not taken that journey first.

The spirit of western humanity has an intrinsic relationship to the Sublime, to spiritual idealism—and this quality was well-recognized in the west even before the advent of Christianity. To the Greeks it was symbolized by the sun-god Apollo, the poet. True Sublimity, however, comes not as an escape from reality or as a fantasy that can be realized with little effort, but as a terrible challenge: the Greeks, though they venerated and invoked him, were terrified of Apollo. We flee the Sublime because it brings to us the image of the consummation of the spiritual life—Heaven itself—and we fear that Heaven might come to us as a reproach, as something we will never be able to live up to.

The west has been Christian for two thousand years, and the essence of Christianity is the Incarnation of God in earthly human form. Consequently our civilization is intrinsically related to the polarity between Spirit and Matter, between the Sublime and the Abyss. In our own time, however, western civilization has turned against the Sublime—which means that the Abyss is all that's left to us now. We saw that the Sublime was capable of producing imbalance and inflation in those exposed to it without sufficient preparation, so we began to believe that it was *only* inflation, nothing but impractical fantasy—what poet Robert Bly in his book *Iron John* called "grandiose ascent". We feared the idea of facing the terrors of our time shielded by nothing but empty idealism. We did not understand, however, that the Sublime, it its terrible aspect, is the very thing that can arm us to meet those terrors. Consequently we fell back into the heavy deadness of materialism. We feared that Sublimity would unground us—but what really caused us to lose our proper ground was the rejection of our own spiritual heritage.

I have written two books about Dante's *Divine Comedy*: *Dark Way to Paradise*, on his *Inferno*; and *The Ordeal of Mercy*, on his *Purgatorio*. *The Divine Comedy* is the greatest poem of Christianity, and also the greatest poem of western civilization. Dante in his master work rendered the Sublime more fully than anyone else in all of western history; but he also showed us the Abyss. And it was his Christianity that allowed him to do this, seeing that Christ descended from Heaven to Earth, died on the cross, harrowed Hell, rose on the third day, and ascended into Heaven where, in the language of the Nicene Creed, he "sits at the right hand of God." And while anyone from any race or nation can be a true Christian, it is also accurate to say that the European soul has an intrinsic affinity for Christ. As Hillaire Belloc and others have shown, Europe was destined for Christ, which is why the European continent could become so completely and organically Christian.

In our own time, however, we have begun the terrible process of rejecting Christ, and consequently have lost our spiritual center. Christ, as the earthly incarnation of God, is the union of Spirit and Matter; so when we reject Christ, we do not just reject the Spirit, but the body as well. We betray the human form. This is not meant to imply that the other revealed religions are any less true in the sight of God, only that the collective soul of western humanity can never be entirely at home in them. When we grab for other spiritual traditions because we have lost or abandoned our own, we often do not receive from them what the natives of those traditions receive, merely a reinforcement of our own materialism. Yoga becomes not a way of union with God but only a form of physical culture; Buddhism is no longer a way of liberation from becoming through the realization of Perfect Total Enlightenment, but a form of atheism that allows us to be "religious" without abandoning any of our materialistic assumptions. We are especially susceptible to this danger when we remain ignorant of our own spiritual tradition. Of course there are many individual exceptions to this rule; nonetheless, spiritual exaltation and the aspiration that goes with it are part of the true character of our civilization; we can't simply deny this by pretending to be a different sort of people than we actually are. To the degree that we have lost touch with our spiritual legacy, the main elements of our cultural essence become inverted, which is one of the very reasons we want to escape them. Loss of cultural identity is thus a vicious circle.

Our intrinsic spirituality, as westerners, leads us beyond our-selves. The down side of this, however, is our collective tendency to lose ourselves in materiality. In this we are very different, for example, from the Taoists of China. For them the spiritual reality of the Tao is not ideally exalted above material conditions, and so the material world is less likely to become a dark gulf that draws them in to their destruction. On the positive side, however, this very polarity between Spirit and Matter, the Sublime and the Abysmal in the western soul, creates a crucible in which an alchemical transmu-tation can take place—and so what ends up being a weakness when the Spirit is denied is revealed as a great strength when the Spirit is accepted. We will tend to run from this split between Spirit and Matter because we fear the problems it can cause, but in running away from it we only widen the split in our own nature. The Spirit cannot be realized until the pull of matter is confronted; in the words of St. Paul, "our strength is perfected in weakness." If we try to embrace the spiritual by simply ignoring the material, we deprive that spirit of all its force and meaning.

Sublimity is essential to the soul of the west, but the ever-present shadow of sublimity is materialism; this is something that Nietzsche understood when he spoke of the tension between the Apollonian and the Dionysian orders. Western civilization, historically speak-ing, has been more immersed in matter than other human collec-tives, therefore the impetus to transcend the material is all the greater; we can see this, for example, both in the somberness of Gre-gorian chant, which gives the impression of a soul in exile crying to God for mercy, and in the great upward thrust of the Gothic arch. And when spiritual aspiration is blocked, this urge to transcend the material produces a great impetus to understand and dominate the material world, to explore all corners of the earth, even to travel through outer space. The soul of the west is sunk in matter and struggling to transcend it; this tension carries with it the potential for matter itself to be spiritualized and redeemed. When the right relationship to the Spirit is achieved, the material world is trans-formed, not abandoned.

If this transformation goes wrong, however, Spirit and body are divorced. We either attempt to live entirely as Spirit, or we try to take refuge in Matter as if it could shield us from Spirit; this may be one of the meanings of the words from the Book of Revelations, "they will pray for the mountains to fall and cover them." But in doing so we fail to recognize how Matter itself is one of the poles of the spiritual life. Matter separated from consciousness is in opposition to the Spirit, but if a conscious light can be turned upon it, Matter can function as a kind of ballast, preventing the spirit from flying away and deserting us. And in another way, the Spirit is a ballast or stabilizing principle for Matter. Without a living relationship to the Spirit, Matter is like a plant that has been severed from its root. Deprived the ballast of the Spirit, which is *form*, Matter returns to formless energy.

When Matter and Spirit are divorced, the mind is darkened; we are pulled either into raw materiality or into the world of fantasy, after which we will be tempted to take refuge in one from the rigors of other—failing to realize that each one actually produces the other. When this divorce first happens, body and Spirit are separated, and a great effort is made to maintain that separation. However, since they are in essence a unity, they are inevitably drawn together again—not in union this time, however, but in conflict. They clash with each other. They try to eat each other up. The thing that is needed to prevent this barren conflict between body and Spirit is what is called, in both alchemy and the New Testament, Salt—and for us in the west, this Salt is Christ: the Spirit made flesh. If we can accept the poles of Spirit and Matter and the tension between them, this can lead to an alchemical transformation of the soul by which it becomes perfectly receptive to the Spirit. And the transformation of the soul transforms the vision of the natural world as well. Thus the ultimate goal of the western tension between the ideal and the material is nothing less than the transfiguration of the cosmos.

The Christian west has traditionally had a more acute sense than other religious collectives that the human soul is fallen. The soul in its fallen state wants to hide from the Spirit, to take comfort and solace in darkness, including the darkness of Matter. Matter, however, is no refuge, because if the Spirit is rejected, the resulting materialism will ultimately lead even to the loss of the body. Without the life of the Spirit we are assailed by fantasy, and fantasy can destroy in us even the sense that we are physical beings, as is amply demonstrated by our contemporary experience of cyberspace. But if the soul can be transfigured by the Spirit, then the body can ultimately be transfigured by the soul; this is one of the inner meanings of the resurrection of the dead. And, although we are rarely aware of it, these transformations are happening within us every day. Dante in his *Commedia* takes us through all the stages of this path of transformation, the journey from the condition of being enmeshed in time and matter, where everything is always deteriorating—from Hell, that is—as far as the station where the body itself has achieved eternal life: the state called Paradise. And it is Christ who presides over this re-marriage of Spirit and body; when such a re-union takes place in the soul, the human person achieves true wholeness and is raised to a higher level of being.

As Dante makes clear, the road from Hell to Paradise, in terms of the Christian way, is a road of Purgation; it requires a struggle against the passions. We all understand what it is to be pulled by the passions, and it is proved to us by the daily news that these passions lead to the degeneration of the quality of *humanity*—the soul, if you will—in the person addicted to them, and finally to the destruction of the circumstances of that person's life, including the body itself. Nonetheless, since an intuition of the Spirit is largely closed to us, we also like to think of the passions as the fullest expression of enthusiasm and vitality; in this we are truly schizophrenic. But if we can feel the pull of the passions, it is also possible to feel the pull of the Spirit. If it were not for the reality of the Spirit within us, the principle of our own integrity, we would not feel the passions of anger and lust and greed and addiction as the assaults upon that integrity that they so obviously are.

If we are not entirely closed to the intuition of the Spirit, we may sometimes be attracted to a "romantic" vision of ancient civilizations as more spiritual than the cultures of today, which is true in many ways. However, the idea that we might find a path to the Spirit hidden within our own still living, though greatly diminished, western tradition has become increasingly implausible to many people. This is because, in our time, the human collective as a whole has turned away from the sense of eternity—consequently individuals who do not accept this rejection of the eternal will find themselves at odds with that collective. They will be looked at as impractical, as mentally imbalanced, even as potential fanatics or terrorists, solely due to their intuition of eternal truth. And this invalidation of the notion of eternity has led to a mass rejection of the entire human past. It used to be said that the fool is the person who was "born yesterday"; by this criterion, all of us are fools.

The attraction of the west to spiritual sublimity is often faulted nowadays for being "other-worldly", as if belief in another world were some kind of guarantee that the believer will hate this world, the earth and the human body. No one, however, who has read the beautiful nature meditations of the monks of the Celtic Church could possibly believe this. But it is true that spiritual sublimity, though it can't be strictly identified with other-worldliness, is certainly related to it; this is because the Sublime can only be fully realized in another world—one that embraces terrestrial existence but is not limited to it. Dante's luminous description of the Terrestrial Paradise at the summit of the Mountain of Purgatory is an expression of this truth. The consciousness of other worlds, higher worlds than this earthly one, can open us to the vision of the Sublime—nor can this vision survive in a climate where these higher worlds are denied. But other-worldliness has a dark side as well. It can open us to metaphysical intuition, but it can also immerse us in destructive fantasy; this is especially true if we are sensitive to the psychic worlds but closed to, or threatened by, the worlds of Spirit. And an attraction to other worlds can certainly also be an over-compensation for a heavy, oppressive materialistic existence. As the alchemical tradition teaches us, however, the Great Work is not simply to spiritualize the body, but also to embody the spirit.

Closely related to other-worldliness, but once again not to be strictly identified with it, is the fascination with death—something that can be considered almost an occupational hazard for lyric or romantic poets. John Keats, for one, spoke of being "half in love with easeful death". An attraction to the mystery of death can be the occasion of a deep confrontation with reality, but it can also lead us astray into various morbid delusions and self-destructive behaviors.

Only those who are firmly grounded in the Spirit can derive real benefit from the contemplation of death.

The goal of the spiritual life is to draw closer to God, to the ultimate Principle of things. The nearer one lives to this Principle, the more fully one occupies eternity, even in this life. Our true duty as human beings is to become absorbed in the eternal, not to grasp after the fleeting remnants of time, or to abandon our spiritual center so as to relate to those chance contemporaries with whom we have only a temporal connection, not an eternal one. If we can accomplish this duty we will find ourselves in communion with all the other embodied souls, of whatever age, who have also finished the Great Work.

We could not live in Paradise
looking on those in Hell
without remaking them
in our own world—
for what we would see
would not be Hell,
but the Paradise of another god.

Made in the USA
Middletown, DE
27 July 2023

35831384R00125